CW00631628

Successful Salon Management

Also from The Macmillan Press

Daniel Galvin   *The World of Hair Colour: the art and techniques of Modern Hair Colouring*

Leo Palladino   *The Principles and Practice of Hairdressing*

Successful Salon Management

Psychology in Hairdressing

ROGER CLIFFE-THOMPSON

Head of Department of Hair and Beauty Studies,
Cannock Chase Technical College,
Cannock

©Roger Cliffe-Thompson 1982

All rights reserved. No part of this publication may be reproduced or transmitted, in any form or by any means, without permission.

First published 1982 by
THE MACMILLAN PRESS LTD
London and Basingstoke
Companies and representatives
throughout the world

Typeset in 11/12pt IBM Journal
by Thames Typesetting,
Abingdon

Printed in Hong Kong

ISBN 0 333 32443 9

CONTENTS

Preface

You've got to be a bit of a psychologist in this game!

There is a strong need within the hairdressing profession for a much greater understanding of human behaviour. Many but not all hairdressers now realise that a high financial profit and a contented clientele and staff are considerably more the results of an appropriate understanding of human behaviour than of a narrow-minded concentration on the mere mechanical aspects of hairdressing. The profession is in need of a book which not only deals with the understanding of why people behave in the way they do but also provides us with ways of controlling what we do so that we can become more efficient.

Psychology is the conscious study of human behaviour. It has formed many sub-disciplines, for example, cognitive psychology studies the workings of the human brain whereas social psychology is concerned with examining the effects of the social and cultural environment on individual behaviour and experience. Now I stress the word 'conscious' because it is the difference in meaning between conscious and unconscious that divides psychology from hairdressing. Psychologists *consciously* study human behaviour whereas hairdressers 'unconsciously' or 'subconsciously' study it and herein lies the reason for this book.

In hairdressing there are certain ways of performing a skill (for example, perming or tinting) which are common to most hairdressers. In addition to these commonly accepted ways there are lots of other ways of, say, sectioning and winding perms, or applying tints, that would achieve the desired result in the long run. However, they would not be as efficient time-wise or in the consumption of materials. If you left an apprentice on her own for a few weeks to work out how to perm a head of hair, she might well succeed and might even

discover the 'accepted' method. But it would be learning by
trial and error, and the one commodity that this method of
learning relies heavily on is time: something we can ill afford to
waste in the salon! So naturally instruction in the skill of hairdressing has become an accepted part of the trade. But what
about social skills? You may have also become naturally skilled
and adept at dealing with people (otherwise you would not be
a hairdresser), but are there more efficient ways of dealing with
others? Can the way you act in a situation affect the human
relations side of your business?

This book attempts to present to you some findings of
psychologists which have *direct application* to your business
and it is hoped that it will help you step back and view your
own behaviour *objectively* and then decide on what specific
strategies to adopt in order to make you a more efficient and
successful hairdresser. Some of the information may appear to
be simply common sense, but the study of human behaviour is
not the prerogative of psychologists alone, and perhaps it will
confirm what you have always felt about people and situations.
But to know that others have studied experimentally the same
phenomena and have come to the same conclusions as yourself
can be very comforting and reassuring. For me one of the main
sources of frustration in hairdressing is that although we are
continually surrounded by people, we tend to be alone when we
have to deal with them.

But remember, we are not trying to turn you into psy-
chiatrists (who mostly study abnormal behaviour) or instant
psychologists. Nor is this book a series of recipes for dealing
with all of life's situations or the exploiting of others. It is
meant simply as a way of presenting some facts and findings
which relate to your own behaviour and that of others, and if
applied, will make the working of your salon more harmonious
and profitable.

As a former salon owner (and now a lecturer) I have for
several years been convinced that a greater understanding of
human psychology can be most beneficial to the hairdresser.
Through my work with the Open University I met some
academic psychologists who were able to translate effectively
what they knew (and had researched) about human behaviour
into a practical form which would be of direct relevance to the
hairdressing profession. Together with these psychologists (in
particular Ray Bull, B.Sc., M.Sc., A.B.Ps.S., and Denis Gahagan,
B.A., A.B.Ps.S., who both wrote major parts of this book) I
organised a considerable number of three-day residential courses

on 'Psychology in Hairdressing' at the University of Notting-
ham. In all, several hundred people attended these courses.
These people came from all parts of the profession—there were
senior managers and managing directors of the largest companies, stylists from the most up-to-date salons, owners of just a
few or one salon, and there were trainees. A frequent request
made at the end of every course was for us to produce a book
incorporating parts of our courses. This we have now done, and
though our courses cover over twenty different topics we have
endeavoured here, in the space available to us, to present information on some of the most important topics. Those wishing to
ask me questions following their reading of this book, or to
enquire about our courses, should feel free to contact me.

I hope that you will enjoy this book.

Roger Cliffe-Thompson

1. An Introduction to Some Psychological Concepts

Memory: how it works and what are its limitations; how best to give instructions to staff

The old joke 'If you can't be a brain surgeon you should be a hairdresser' may not be so far removed 'physically' from the truth as it seems. Apart from hatters (who have all gone mad anyway) I can think of no other profession which deals with the human head day in and day out, working only half an inch away from that most unique feature, the human brain. The brain is an incredible product of evolution that manages to synthesise a whole range of complex physiological and psychological tasks without any conscious effort, thus leaving the individual free to practise the skills necessary for survival in a social world.

But the brain cannot function without information. If deprived, it will start to manufacture its own, with strange results. Experiments have been performed on 'sensory deprivation' wherein volunteers have been literally wrapped in cottonwool, given ear muffs and blindfolded. Many people could not take more than half an hour or so in these conditions, and those that did often reported weird experiences and sensations which felt frighteningly real. To obtain information the brain relies on a number of input channels which are remarkable for their sensitivity and ability to change all sorts of stimuli into chemical signals.

The eyes, for example, translate a three-dimensional, multi-coloured visual signal into a series of electrochemical pulses which travel from the front of the head to the back via the optic nerve.
The ears pick up vibrations which are translated by the brain into meaningful sounds.

1

The nose and mouth transmit taste and smells, while pressure receptors all over the body are transmitting a sensation of *touch,* bodily comfort and muscular co-ordination.

All these channels transmit a virtually never-ending stream of signals and the brain sorts it all out, performing calculations and sending out instructions to the body millions of times a second. Perhaps it is worth considering for a moment just a fraction of the information that is being processed and acted upon almost subconsciously by you at this very moment.

While you are reading this, try to concentrate on your body. Can you feel the touch of the clothes next to your skin? How comfortable is the chair you are sitting upon? How long could you sit on it before shifting in your seat? What about your legs, are they crossed or uncrossed? If so can you feel the pressure of one across the other? If not, can you feel the chair cutting in behind your knees? When will you consciously have to decide to move them? Listen to your breathing, *in... out....* How much time would you have left for other things if you had to remind yourself to breath in, then out, every few seconds? What about noises around you? Can you focus on them and identify them? Traffic? Hairdryers? Children playing? Vacuum cleaners working?

Now concentrate on this passage and try to work out your weekly staff/client ratio, that is, take the number of staff you employ, including apprentices; then add up approximately how many clients you process every day, add them together to get a weekly total then divide by the number of staff employed including yourself.

Clients processed:	Monday	
	Tuesday	
	Wednesday	
	Thursday	
	Friday	
	Saturday	_____
	Total	_____
	Divide	
	by no. of	
	staff	_____
	=	_____

What has happened to all that other information I asked you to concentrate on? Hasn't it just faded away? Isn't it remarkable how you can single-mindedly carry out a task and exclude all other distractions? Of course it depends to a certain extent on how interesting the task becomes for you. For example, try and winkle a junior out of the staffroom while she's reading a magazine, or, conversely, see how important other distractions, such as mirror-cleaning or floor-brushing, become when the last client of the day arrives, late, for her shampoo and set. However, if the input from one channel is too great, then it can seriously hamper your ability to carry out a task. Have you ever tried, for example, to concentrate on a hair style while someone is working with a road drill outside the salon?

Concentration is related to motivation and other psychological functions, most of which take place in the cerebral cortex. The immense development of this part of the brain has given us our uniquely human artistic and aesthetic qualities and has been the main reason for the human species' rise to dominance over the rest of the animal kingdom. The brain is also responsible for storing and relating past experience to new problems. Many of the problems in the salon concern memory. It is amazing, is it not, how members of staff can forget and become muddled about things which to you are a simple set of instructions? Yet they can remember to the last penny, how much commission they earned last week.

Perhaps you would care to test your memory now. Try looking at the following set of numbers and for a period of about thirty seconds commit them to memory.

$$5 \quad 1 \quad 6 \quad 3 \quad 9 \quad 7 \quad 2 \quad 3 \quad 6$$

Now jot down the name of the woman who gave King Charles the oranges:

. . .   .

Now read on.

The brain will filter and select information and this selection will depend on your past experience and perception of the situation, dictating how you deal with the situation. How we perceive other people and situations can vary drastically from society to society. In our society we can be prone to 'perceiving' situations in a very strange way indeed. Take surrealism, for example. Perhaps Ernst with his 'sit up and beg' coffin is pointing a finger at the surrealistic way we enclose bodies (in wood and brass) before burying them in a hole which is then covered with a slab of marble. Why bury them lying down, why not sitting up? Or see how Salvador Dali turns the face of Mae

West into a stage setting and transforms her lips into a couch. One of the main functions of the surrealists seems to be turning objects into things which they are not.

But does surrealism only exist in art? Do you remember 'happy tenderness day darling', an advertisement that appeared on the television not so long ago, where the wife appeared walking down the corridor carrying a silver platter, on which rested the roasted remains of a poor lamb, its ribs decorated with chefs' hats? 'Happy *tenderness* day darling', she calls to her husband! Another advertisement asked us to believe that a brand of petrol could actually metamorphose into an animal. You don't believe me? Remember 'Put a tiger in your tank'? Perhaps our society needs surrealism; certainly there can be nothing more surrealistic than the things we do to hair in our profession. Consider, for example, the chemical hydrogen peroxide. In the salon it changes and becomes a 'brightener'. After a perm it becomes a 'neutraliser' (it's a wonder vets don't use it). Similarly, when perming, ammonium thioglycollate can be called 'tailored curl' or 'spring curl'. Or clients ask for a 'body wave' (perhaps this one originated during the Spanish Inquisition). Or they ask for a 'light perm'. 'Certainly, madam. 60 or 100 watts?' We also tell them that it will give their hair a little 'bounce' or 'life'. But seriously, there is a very good reason for using surrealistic expressions in hairdressing. Certainly, some clients would run a mile if they suspected the true nature of some of the processes we use on them. On the other hand, they might rather not know, preferring to leave the whole thing in our competent hands. The expressions we use also tend to soften and add associated feelings to our product. Nevertheless, it is an interesting point that although we know that the active ingredient in a neutraliser is hydrogen peroxide, junior staff who have never had it explained to them haven't a clue what it contains, and if we don't explain carefully the meaning of our terminology to staff, we cannot blame them if they make a simple mistake because they didn't understand fully the way hairdressing processes work.

Talking about processes and the way they work, what about your memory process? How is it working? Just jot down the numbers you were earlier asked to commit to memory.

. . . .

By the way, what was the name of that woman we also asked about?

.. . .

Compare your numerical answers with the originals on p.3. How did you score? Did you get all or any of the numbers correct? Were any of them in the correct order?

Past experience has shown that the majority of people have little difficulty remembering names but have varying degrees of difficulty with the recall of numbers.

Think back and try to decide what strategy you adopted when you committed the numbers to memory. How did you handle the information? Did you try to remember all nine figures in their original sequence? Or did you break the numbers up into smaller groups, for example, three blocks of three: 516, 397, 236? Or two and three and four: 51, 639, 7236? Or did you add the numbers together to make nine: $5 + 1 = 6$, $6 + 3 = 9$, $9 = 9$, $7 + 2 = 9$? Or did you use a completely different strategy from any of these?

Now questions that I find interesting are:

(1) If there are so many strategies that can be adopted, are some more efficient than others?
(2) If I remember them all, is there any general limit to the sequences of numbers that I can remember?
(3) Why in general is it easier to remember names (which often contain more than nine letters) as opposed to a list of nine figures?
(4) Finally, is there any way of making remembering easier?

However, though these questions are interesting you are probably wondering about their relevance to the salon situation. I agree, so let's look at some classic examples. *Frizzy perms:* are they not often the result of staff forgetting to check the process at regular intervals? (Or worse still, forgetting about the client completely!) *Broken bleaches:* highlights can break off if for the same reason the bleach is left on for too long. And who hasn't suddenly remembered those highlights under the dryer, whipped them over to the sink, rinsed them, then with bated breath combed ever so gently through the tangle of fragile white 'worms' praying none stay on the comb! Or conversely, what about under-processing? How about the perm that inexplicably takes ages? Until you discover that *somebody* has mixed up your instructions and diluted the perm lotion by three to one instead of one to one, as you had asked! Or the junior who brings three unsweetened coffees and four sugared teas instead of three unsweetened teas and four sugared coffees? Some of the consequences of these examples of memory lapses are small, some are large. But all are irritating, time-wasting and in the long run can cost money. So what about those four questions we asked earlier? Psychology can provide an answer. Experimental psychologists have for a long time been studying the way that memory works and one of the most substantiated findings to date is entitled 'The magic number 7 plus or minus 2' (which is written 7-2). This theory proposes that the maximum amount of information that most of us can handle (in order to be able to remember it) is seven pieces, give or take two. That is, some people can remember five pieces of information while others can remember nine. But what are 'pieces' of information? It seems that as long as the information is a whole then a piece can either be a number or a letter, that is, 1 or 9 (which psychologists call 'bits') or it can be a word (for example, Nell) which is called a 'chunk'. So obviously by converting data into 'pieces' you can get a lot more into the memory store than you can via bits. This is why, for me, the GPO made it much harder when they changed their telephone codes from words into numbers: Mossley Hill 9437 was much easier to remember than 051 724 9437, because there are two chunks and four bits in the first example making a total of six items of data. In the second instance there are ten bits, that is, a total of ten items of data, so obviously the first example, according to the magic 7-2 theory, has a much better chance of being retained. In the salon, therefore, it is not surprising that some staff find it much easier to remember permanent colours by their name, rather than their number. And if you ask them to fetch more than two colours by referring to them by number, then the more chance there is of them getting mixed up.

But to return to the bits and pieces. When the information is carried to the brain via the senses it is collected in a short-term store and it is then processed by what is called 'a selective filter'. This is what enabled you to perform the calculation of your staff/client ratio, and successfully ignore other irrelevant stimuli. I presume that if I ask you what that ratio was, you will be able to answer, whereas if I asked you to list the sounds you heard during your calculations of the figure you would probably have a problem in remembering much about them. So the selective filter plays a role concerning whether information is remembered and it is best represented by the following diagram:

SENSES ⟶ SHORT-TERM STORE ⟶ SELECTIVE FILTER ⟶ FORGOTTEN

LONG-TERM STORE

But what about the strategies we mentioned? If, for example, I had told you that the sequence of numbers was actually a telephone number, would you have handled it differently? Past experience in dealing with telephone numbers would probably have helped you remember it more efficiently. What about Nell Gwynne? Her name was deliberately selected because it's a name which means something to most people and is already in our long-term memory store. Therefore it can more easily be recalled, whereas the name Anne Ravel might easily have been forgotten. So the strategies that you adopt, or the way the information is presented can have a positive effect on whether it is remembered or not.

In our case the number sequence presented to you had nine bits (the top end of the magic 7-2), so it would not be surprising if you recalled part of the sequence incorrectly. (If you did get it all correct, take a pat on the back and I will send you all our telephone numbers to remember!) In the case of Nell Gwynne the nine letters were packaged into two words, so they went into the memory store as two chunks. It's not surprising therefore that you had little difficulty recalling her name. If you did have difficulty then you are either a strict moralist or the section on surrealism worked wonderfully well, because, as you've probably guessed by now, it was deliberately used as a distraction in that we attempted to subject you to a different kind of stimulus—humour.

Of course all these distractions are continuously happening in your salon. If you give a member of staff a set of complex instructions, don't be surprised if they fail to carry them out. A junior, for example, may be thinking about what she is going to wear for that new date tonight, or may be harrassed by the demands of more than one member of staff. Distractions may also occur when more senior members of staff become caught up with a problem on the telephone while they are in the middle of a process. Thus to answer one of the foregoing questions, the best strategy to adopt when giving instructions is

*"You juniors are all the same. You seem incapable of
remembering all the useful things I tell you."*

to write instructions in a simple list form. However, if you
cannot do this, then:

(1) try not to give out more than five pieces of instruction
(which will allow the minimum number of chunks to be
remembered);

(2) make the task logical (that is, build up the sequence into
what is known); for example, rather 'First get the perm
lotion and then the neutraliser', than 'First get the
neutraliser and then the perm lotion';

(3) try to relate the information to past experience; for
example, 'You remember how we used diluted perm
lotion on Mrs Fazackerley's hair; well, do exactly the
same this time, use 1 oz. of lotion to 2 oz. of water.'

Finally, perhaps next time you dress a client's hair, it may
well be worth remembering the incredible amount of activity

that is going on in your head and also a fraction of an inch away from your fingertips. Yet it's also worth considering that clients have active brains as well and we shall come to discuss the importance of what they think later.

Creativity: how to be more creative

Hairdressers have always stressed the creative aspect of the craft. Yet ask any hairdresser to define or outline what creativity is and they will probably find difficulty in answering your question. If you go one stage further and ask them how to be creative, or to tell you how they go about becoming creative, you will probably have difficulty in getting any sort of answer. The problem is that creativity is one of those things that at times is impossible to describe until you have been creative (for example, when trying to design a totally new hairstyle, you cannot describe it before you have created it — otherwise, if you could, it would not be a new hairstyle). At other times it is impossible to be creative because all the factors which go together to put you in a creative mood are not present.

Although perhaps it is difficult to define creativity, it may be possible to define some of the areas which help towards making creativity. You may question why a section on creativity is included in this book. But I hope that this section will have a twofold effect in that (1) it may greatly affect the way that you use the material in this book, and (2) in its own right it may affect your approach to the dozens of little problems that crop up from day to day in your business which require a creative approach.

The creative process

Everybody has creative potential, the problem is that most of the time it is inhibited. It is inhibited to a large extent by the physical world we live in. Most people who live in two-storey houses sleep upstairs and only a tiny minority reverse that living arrangement. It may be more convenient to sleep upstairs; but for the majority, they do it because it is the conventional thing to do, and conforming to what is 'normal' is a very powerful force in our society. Similarly you may be unadventurous in the way you travel to work every morning, but this might not be because you are conforming to group norms, but rather that you find getting a lift from your front door every morning the most economical (petrol-saving) and time-saving method of getting to work. But let there be an oil shortage or rationing become adopted, and see how quickly you become creative about solving the problem of getting to work. You might consider jogging, walking, the bus, the train, biking or even altering work hours to suit transport times. In this case, how creative you are will depend upon how much you want to solve the problem; for example, if all petrol tanker drivers went on strike, you probably wouldn't search too seriously for a solution. You know that the government will intervene and the *status quo* will be resumed fairly quickly. But should your regular lift sell the car because of the escalating price of petrol, then it's fairly certain that you will search long and hard for serious alternatives.

But this is only one problem. The purpose of this section is to equip you with ways of solving various types of problem as they occur in different ways. Think, for example, how you would go about making a piece of sculpture to display in your salon. Would you (1) build it up by adding clay to clay, or (2) chip away at a piece of stone until you arrived at a shape? Both would fulfil the same function but be arrived at by entirely different routes and it is the way we think about problems that can be of immense importance. This whole book is designed to enhance the way you think about your job.

Convergent thinking

The way we are brought up in our society tends to direct us to thinking convergently (that is, we have become used to dealing with problems that have only one solution). Mathematical solutions to many problems are simple and often easy to arrive at, so we tend to use the same techniques when approaching other problems. Take, for example, the operator who comes and tells you: 'Mrs Jones is in and I can't find any perm lotion X for her perm.' The standard reply from you is: 'Well use perm lotion Y'. 'But Mrs Jones always has X.' In order to find a solution to this problem you go into the dispensary, pour some perm lotion Z which is the same colour as X into an old empty X bottle and return with, 'Here, use this.' A couple of hours later the operator will probably inform you that 'Mrs Jones was delighted with her perm and gave me a large tip. See, I told you there was nothing like lotion X.' So there you have it, the classic case of convergent thinking from the operator — but *divergent* thinking from you. *Divergent* thinking is where you go outside the normal, standard answer; where you question the restraints. Why should Mrs Jones always have the same perm lotion? Why should Mrs Jones even have the same operator? Why not another one who perms superbly with lotion *Y*? Why should Mrs Jones have a perm at all today? Why not a restyle with highlights? The only constraint on your approach to the problem is the fact that Mrs Jones is booked in and (1) has an expectation that some form of major process is going to happen to her hair, and (2) she expects to spend a larger amount than normal with you.

Areas and constraints

Ask yourself, am I prepared to look for other areas in which I can solve the problem? Is it worth the bother? For example, the new junior I have taken on — she's useless, sits around smoking, she's been with me for ten weeks now, I only kept her on because she's a daughter of a friend and though she's very pleasant, she hasn't got a clue. Still she'll be gone in two weeks. I know she'll be disappointed, but she'll be off my hands and I can always say I tried. End of approach to problem. Or is it? What about the public relations aspect? What if you were to look at the problem again? Try to redirect her career — give her days off to look at other areas or persuade the girl to give *her* notice in or get her mother to come in and have her hair done and let the lass shampoo her? Ask yourself *what are the constraints* within which we must work? Sit down and define them. Actually write down the constraints. You'll probably be astonished by how few there really are. For example, your salon needs restyling and the obvious constraints may be (1) expense—money available; (2) the colour scheme mustn't be too drastic; (3) time/inconvenience — it can't be done in working hours; (4) the placement of fittings, basins, dryer banks, etc., may constrain you; (5) will the clients/staff like it?

Let's take them in order:

(1) Expense — a complete restyling of the salon with extra equipment may cost more, but it may (a) bring in new custom, and (b) allow you to raise prices thus paying for itself. In this light is the original cash limit so important?

(2) New colour schemes are difficult and consulting another source can be very useful, from the professional to getting a selection of hairdressing journals with pictures

of salon decor and involving the staff and clients by
asking their preferences. This may completely invalidate
the initial constraints that you had (for example, that the
staff and clients may not like it).

(3) Time, a real constraint this one: but instead of rushing
into it and having it done *now* why not deliberately
arrange to have all materials ordered, professionals
booked and close completely for, say, the second week in
January when business may be at its quietest. Or do it in
two separate stages over long weekends.

(4) Finally, fixtures and fittings — are they as fixed as you
initially thought? Would it take so much effort to move a
dryer bank and have an extra row of sockets fitted.
Could you do without that drying bay now that a lot of
blowdrying is being done: could you use the space for
other things?

In other words, examine first, what are the constraints within
which I must work? Second, how fixed are these constraints?
Third, is there another way of looking at the problems I face?
Fourth, am I prepared to go outside or around the constraints?
Psychologists have found that when these questions are asked
many efficient, satisfactory and profitable results are often
produced.

Apart from the constraints within which I must work, what
about those relating to myself.

(1) *The fear of failing or being frustrated:* how often have
you not attempted a task because you were worried
about looking a fool if you failed?

(2) *Rigidity:* how conventional are you? In a way, this one is
related to convergent thinking. Don't the old answers to
the problem just seem to be the best because they're old?

(3) *Over-seriousness:* this can not only relate to fear of
failing, but it can also occur because the problem has
been blown up out of all proportion and the consequences, should you fail, may appear to be enormous.

(4) *Dullness of emotions:* many people try to solve problems
immediately, or at the end of a working day. Ask yourself whether you are doing yourself justice in seeking an
answer by approaching it physically and mentally exhaus-
ted. The old adage 'sleep on it' is certainly useful. One
company undertook a study in which they instructed all
staff to wait at least forty-eight hours before they ans-

wered any problem (agreed, it would be virtually impossible in hairdressing) but apparently it was a huge success.

(5) *Submissiveness:* perhaps this one is the most lethal of all.
'Oh, there's nothing I can do about it', or 'They will win
anyway.' It usually relates to points (3) and (4) above.
Hang it — get stuck in — be resourceful and above all be
imaginative.

Let your imagination help you solve problems. Consider
the following:

(1) *Significance:* see it from other people's point of view.
How significant or real is the problem to them?

(2) *Introspection:* go inside the problem, examine it in detail;
are there any parts that have become so obvious to you
that you have overlooked them?

(3) *Change of perspective:* try to view the problem from a
different standpoint (for example, that of a cat or giraffe)
or consult others.

(4) *Inversion:* turn it upside down; it may look ridiculous but
it may also give fresh insight.

(5) *Time dimension:* how will the problem appear in three
months? It may have faded away, so stop worrying about
it. It may sometimes become worse and in that case ACT
NOW before it's too late.

So you see to a certain extent you have put a logical
structure on creativity! Once you have practised these different
techniques and applied them to different situations you will
probably find that they can be used in all sorts of ways, but
perhaps the main advantage of performing any or all of these
exercises is that it very quickly enables you to become objective
about any situation. I cannot stress too much the necessity of
being able to be objective about all management problems. The
difference between objective and subjective is epitomised in
the phrase, 'you can't see the wood for the trees' (that is, your
own perception of the situation governs your response). A
typical example is when you are trying to persuade a junior
member of staff to either demonstrate on stage or model a new
hairstyle. You may be met with the oft-repeated phrase, 'I
can't, everybody will be looking at me'. Again the junior is
allowing her subjective views to govern her response. Often
she will be deaf to your *objective* reasoning; for example,
'Don't be silly, there will be twenty other people on the stage;

why should anyone be looking at you in particular!'

"That way of doing it always worked in the past, but it failed this time. Now I've no idea what else to try!"

In conclusion I hope that you have found this section on creativity interesting and, more important, I hope it affects the ways that you view the contents of the rest of this book.

Gain and loss of esteem and its effect on staff

We all like to be liked and one of the major factors in deciding whether or not you like a person is how that other person behaves towards you (Chapter 2, on first impressions, will also bear on this point).

Since the early 1950s social psychologists have investigated this 'liking' concept and have found that if you consider the other person's behaviour to be 'rewarding' you will tend to like them. The reward mainly lies in the other person's attitude towards you being expressed in positive feelings and opinions, but if they express negative feelings and say derogatory things about you, then you will probably dislike them. This seems straightforward and more or less common sense, but even here there are questions to be asked. If you want clients and staff to like you, does it mean to say that you have to be constantly friendly and say nice things to everybody all of the time? Consider what happens when the pressures on staff are high: it's a hot day and the clients seem to be more demanding than ever. You don't smile at a client, you snap at the junior — is that it? Will they now automatically dislike you? Or conversely, you are not the sort of person who gushes at everybody, you're sincere and prefer to get to know people before you say anything about anybody. Does this mean you won't be a success with people?

There are a number of relevant factors here concerning (1) the difference in the way people are nice to others; (2) the difference in the way people consider others are being nice to them.

In 1965 two experimental social psychologists put forward a notion that it was the feeling of whether you had gained or lost the esteem of the other person which affected your attitude to them and not, as one might think, that liking a person depends simply on the total number of times that they were nice to you. More interestingly, they also proposed:

(1) that you will tend to like a person even more if their attitude towards you gradually increases from being negative to becoming increasingly positive; and
(2) if that person becomes negative towards you after a positive start it has a far more punishing effect than if they were negative to you to begin with.

Here (1) refers to a gain in esteem, (2) to a loss in esteem. We might ask how this concept can be applied to hairdressing. Well, let's look at our own behaviour towards others. First think of your normal everyday self — the *real* you. Now examine the graph in Figure 1 and look across at the line which says Norm. Now think of your attitude and behaviour on the morning when you start a new member of staff. How far above or below that norm line are you?

Remember the graph refers to *your* behaviour and the words we have selected — effusive, hostile, etc. — describe a graduation in behaviour away from the normal you. So although you may not be an aloof person as such, still use the line where 'aloof' is to indicate when you are displaying the sort of behaviour just before you become hostile. (The numbers 1,2, 3,4, etc., can be used to represent any period of time, that is, days, months, etc., and are there only to make a clear pattern over time.)

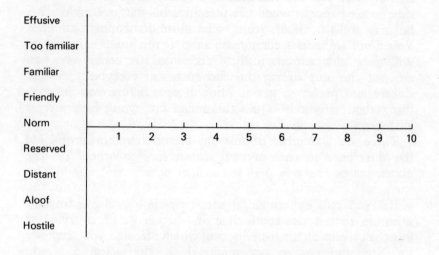

Figure 1 Gain and loss of esteem and its effect on staff

Most people say, when starting a new member of staff, that they will be above the norm line. Some hairdressers have told me that on reflection, they are extremely effusive, beaming, fussing, etc. Others have said that they become extremely aloof, feeling that they don't want to appear as if they are fussing. No matter, put a cross by the attitude which you think you adopt, above or below the 0. Now think of yourself on the morning exactly one week later. How is your attitude expressed to that week-old staff now? Has it changed at all? Or are you still behaving towards him/her in a similar way? Put a cross above or below 1 in the position that indicates your attitude towards that person after one week. So now think of your behaviour towards them on a morning of the second week. You must know them a little better by now; has this affected your behaviour yet? Are you still over-friendly (compared to your norm) or has your attitude changed slightly? No matter, plod on. Fill in a cross above 2. Now it's the start of the third week: how is your behaviour now? Fill in with a cross at the appropriate level on 3. Fourth week, any change? Fill it in above 4. At the beginning of the fifth week, they have been with you one full month. Any change? Remember your behaviour is compared to your normal behaviour towards others — yes or no? Fill it in above 5.

Not long to go now, the beginning of the sixth week: they've settled in *or* you may be unhappy with their performance and have sacked them (never mind, put a cross in the hostile place beneath 6 and just read on), or you're still happy but other events are of much more immediate significance (like a hefty rate demand) and you may be returning to normal — or you may still be continuing the 'honeymoon'. Whatever, put the cross against 6. Week seven: any change? Put a cross against 7. Week eight? Put the cross against 8. Finally, week nine: they have been with you nine weeks so put a cross above or below 9.

We're now going to examine the different types of graph (see figure 2) people might end up with and with which you can match yours.

Your graph should fit roughly into one of these (that is, the patterns should go straight as in (1) and (2), or dip drastically as in (3), or curve downwards or upwards as in (4) and (5)). If your graph doesn't look like any of these, then still read on. I'm sure you will work something out.

Now let us examine the implications that each pattern of behaviour contains. Graphs (1) and (2) show that consistently for nearly ten weeks you have behaved towards that new member of staff in a way that is *not* the normal you. Now then, if you follow this type of pattern, you have set up a certain expectancy in that new member of staff of a way of behaving towards them! How long are you going to be able to keep it up? Just put a X at norm level after 10 in graph (1) and now look at graph (1) again. As soon as you behave normally towards that member of staff, they are going to think that they have lost a lot of your esteem. So what's going to happen? Are you going to let them think that you don't like them all of a sudden (you've been extra nice to them for ten weeks as far as they are concerned and now you are not)? They are obviously going to try to rationalise your behaviour towards them, and the normal answer they will come up with is that they have done something wrong or something to offend you and, since they haven't, there is obviously going to be a conflict situation. Or realising that you have set up this expectation, are you going to try to maintain your new behaviour? It's going to be hard work!

Conversely, let's look at graph (2). Again put a cross after 10 on the norm line. Now you will see that your behaviour

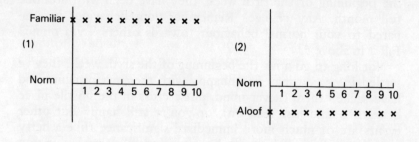

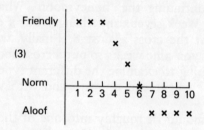

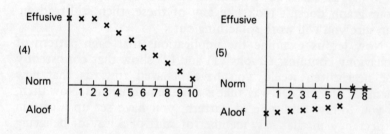

Figure 2 Behaviour patterns

towards them has jumped from ten weeks of negative to one week of a positive attitude. They will consider this a large reward from you because your esteem for them has gone from negative to positive. They again will try to rationalise this new piece of behaviour from you, and will probably assume that they are performing much better than they are. Is this the impression you intended to create? The only hope you have of maintaining the *status quo* is to keep on being reserved, but can your really keep this up for ever more? Funnily enough, hairdressers have told me that graph (1) can explain why some apprentices walk out after three months. The apprentices said they left because the boss suddenly didn't like them ('the manager wasn't speaking nicely to me any more'). Graph (1) also shows why a member of staff could not understand recent criticisms of her work — 'You've been nice to me for the last few weeks.' Graph (3) could explain why a person feels so bitter about being sacked. It's not the loss of a job but the unexplained loss of esteem. Starting off near your normal and then dropping to it would have been a much smaller drop in esteem. In graph (3) the drop may be huge because you started away up on a false level of over-friendly then plummeted. Obviously the member of staff will try to rationalise the event and, because it appears unexplainable in any other way, they will think it is a reflection on their own inability to work, which may or may not be true. Graph (4) perhaps shows one of the most commonplace patterns, in that there appears to be a gradual cooling off of your initially favourable attitude. The effect is the same as graph (1) and (3) only to a much lesser extent, since the loss of esteem is gradual over a period of weeks. Nevertheless, it could still have a detrimental effect since the member of staff has to explain the loss of esteem. They could easily become cynical about you and express such remarks as, 'Yes, the manager's all over you at first. I wondered when the honeymoon would be over, still he/she's like that with everyone when they start... Now what I say is...'

Graph (5) works in the opposite way, in that apparently it rewards the new member of staff, but in much smaller doses than in graph (2), allowing the past week's behaviour to become the norm, so that any one week's move towards normal doesn't appear so significant. Also it's easier for you to relax and not have to monitor yourself continuously. This behaviour pattern would seem to be one which would (a) produce the least anxiety in staff; (b) be the easiest for you to cope with; and (c) produce the most beneficial result in the terms of good staff relationships. Thus, according to the theory *it is most effective to move gradually from a negative attitude to a more positive one.* However, if you disagree with this it does not matter, the exercise is still valuable in that it will make you look at your own initial approach to new members of staff and clients in a more objective way.

In what way can the deliberate use of loss of esteem be of benefit in salon management? Well, there are times in a salon when staff behaviour is not all that it should be. It may be useful to use 'loss of esteem' as a way of reinforcing more desirable behaviour. For example, place a cross on the norm column above 0 in figure 3. Now plot the graph for your responses in relation to the following sequence of behaviour

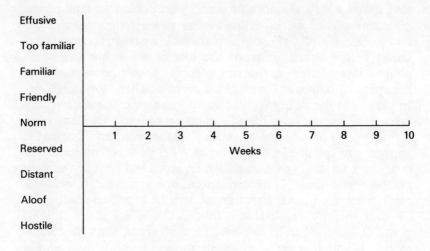

Figure 3

from a member of staff:

  (1) staff elicits an undesirable piece of behaviour — place a cross against 'distant' under 1;
  (2) staff elicits desirable piece of behaviour — reward by moving a cross to 'norm' under 2;
  (3) staff elicits an undesirable piece of behaviour — place a cross against 'distant' under 3;
  (4) staff elicits a further piece of undesirable behaviour — place a cross against 'aloof' under 4;
  (5) staff elicits desirable piece of behaviour — place a cross against 'distant' under 5;
  (6) staff elicits desirable piece of behaviour — place a cross against 'norm' under 6;
  (7) staff elicits extraordinarily good behaviour — reward by placing a cross against 'friendly' above 7;
  (8) staff elicits normal behaviour — place a cross halfway between 'friendly' and 'norm' above 8 in order to lessen effect of apparent loss of esteem;
  (9) staff elicits normal behaviour — place a cross on 'norm' above 9 — carry on as normal.

There are obviously all sorts of variations in the ways that this theory can be used, but perhaps the main advantages are that it allows *you* to view your behaviour objectively and use normal behaviour which is easy to maintain, rather than abnormal behaviour which is hard to maintain, to help regulate

"You've been here 6 weeks now and I have always been nice to you. But now I am going to have to tell you off!"

your relationship with staff.

Finally, the concept of gain and loss of esteem doesn't only apply to staff relationships. It can be used in all sorts of situations. Take clients, for example. The 'taken-for-granted syndrome' where a client of long standing abruptly stops attending your salon, or starts becoming very demanding, can easily be explained by graph (4). The initial extra attention that the client received as a new client has dwindled down to 'normal' attention. So the client who tries to understand 'why' either tries to return to her 'norm' of service *she* experienced at the beginning by becoming more demanding, or she feels that she is being taken for granted and leaves altogether. Again if an operator continuously tells a client, at the end of the service, how marvellous her hairstyle is, then obviously they are initiating graph (1), and as the 'marvellous' expression at the end of the process becomes the norm, then it has to be maintained, or risk the loss of esteem (that is, if at the end of the next session the 'marvellous' comment and appropriate behaviour were not forthcoming, the client may not only be disappointed but feel unconsciously that her hairstyle is far worse than it really is).

By maintaining a *normal* relationship with a client, it allows you to occasionally give esteem without the dangers of loss. For example, if a client requests a special coiffure for a wedding, you can give her that extra amount of attention and tell her how wonderful she looks on that occasion, without building up the expectation of similar treatment every time. In fact you *reward* her for asking for a special service. So the chances are that she won't hesitate in spending a little more with you the next time a special occasion arises. In other words you build up another set of *norms* of behaviour for special occasions.

In conclusion, the implications of this concept are to make yourself aware of what is your own norm (people differ) and then briefly move above and below it as the situation demands. The rule is 'be thyself by knowing thyself'! If you do this you can relax yet react to the situation when it is required.

Audience effects: what having an audience does to the hairdresser's performance

How often have you stopped to watch a junior perming or completing a hairstyle, only to be told, 'Go away you're making me nervous'? On the other hand, how often when rehearsing for a show, or practising for a competition have you heard the words, 'Oh it will be alright on the night'? In the first instance the inference is that watching someone will affect their work adversely, yet in the second case it's as if they are actively seeking an audience to make them perform better. Psychologists have been concerned with why the mere presence of others has effects on our behaviour. What happens, for example, if you suddenly suspect someone is watching you while you are eating? – does it make you uneasy? How do you feel when you walk alone into a room full of strange people – do you become very conscious of your appearance and start touching your clothes or hair?

'Audience effects', as they have become known, have been studied since the end of the nineteenth century when a psychologist, studying the effects of putting pacers in with racing cyclists while they were training, found that their performance improved much more when they were working alone than with someone else. But the major study which really started a host of experiments into audience effects was one undertaken in Chicago in the 1930s. The 'Hawthorne effect' resulted from a series of small studies undertaken at the Hawthorne works of the American General Electric Company. To begin with the researchers decided to study the effects which altering the illumination had on the efficiency of workers assembling and checking electrical components. Surprisingly, it was observed that not only did the output of workers given better lighting improve, but so also did that of another group given no such advantages. To check the accuracy of their results, a follow-up study was undertaken which even more surprisingly demonstrated that even when lighting was reduced to the equivalent of *moonlight,* the two women selected for the study still maintained high levels of production. Clearly the levels of lighting were not responsible for the improvement in performance, and in an attempt to try to find the cause for the improvement a further series of experiments was devised in which a variety of other factors were altered. But nearly all the strategies adopted were met by increased productivity. The surprise came when they observed that the complete removal of all the improvements they had made was still accompanied by further increases in performance!

It was not until some time later that it was realised that the only factor which was common to all studies that would explain the results was one that had previously been totally ignored: the fact that the people knew they were being studied. Since then there have been a host of further experiments which have shown that as far as skills are concerned, the notion that an audience facilitates performance has been well supported. This would seem to explain why actors come good on the night. But what of your junior? It certainly does not explain his/her apprehension and poor performance! Read on...

One psychologist presented people with a particular passage and a pair of words, and the subjects were then required to select the word that they believed to be more consistent with the passage. Subjects' decisions were timed in each of three experimental conditions: (1) deciding alone, except for an experimenter; (2) deciding before an audience of other students and a faculty member who could be seen on the other side of a window; and (3) deciding before an unseen audience, previously described to the subject, on the other side of a one-way window.

On average, decision times were shortest for subjects who were alone and longest for subjects performing before an unseen audience. The observable audience condition fell between these two. So the kind of audience seemed to play an important role in the overall effect and since it was the unseen audience which *inhibited* the people's performance, it seems that not knowing the capability of your audience may cause an undesirable effect. Let's analyse this 'unknown' factor a little further. It would seem that, because the audience is unknown, you may well think that part of the audience may consist of people who have more specialist knowledge or skill than yourself. If this is so, it is understandable that any future action by you is likely to be inhibited (that is, you will want to make absolutely sure that either the decision you make is the correct one, or that the skill you are demonstrating is done correctly). So now we are going some way to explaining why that junior gets nervous when working in front of you. They think that you will see every mistake they make. You of course are probably just offering parental friendliness and if the truth were known you had really spotted only a few mistakes.

A further explanation is that the complexity of the task performed also has a crucial bearing on the result. It was noted that the performance which was improved by the audience effect involved tasks requiring *well-learned behaviour.* Performance that was inhibited by audience effects involved the acquisition of new information *during* the task.

The obvious implication that can be drawn from this in relation to hairdressing is that if you want staff to perform skills in front of an audience, then they must practise the skill until they have mastered it. In this way they will perceive their audience to be less capable than they, and therefore they will display their technique to the full. The danger lies in deviating on the night from any plan and suddenly asking or expecting staff to perform in areas they have not practised. *It could turn into a shambles.* There are certain people who appear to be able to put on a display or show 'off the cuff', but like Morecambe and Wise the best off-the-cuff material is well rehearsed. Audience effects could also explain why a junior who has entered for a competition suddenly decides for some inexplicable reason in the middle of the competition to do something completely different and usually ends up with a complete disaster.

The same concepts apply in such diverse areas as speech-making (that is, always rehearse well), or moving junior staff on to more complex tasks, or deciding whether or not you will ever go back to using cubicles instead of open plan (it may come, you never know!). According to the theory, people should work slower when they're isolated in cubicles than when they are working with other people in an open-plan situation.

However there would be nothing to stop you using glass sides to the cubicle; in that way the audience would be present but it would not intrude on the performance (for example, by gossip).

Finally, there is one other interesting theory about audience effects and this is that the mere presence of others often represents a source of comfort or support in the face of anxiety. In one experiment, student subjects who were awaiting their turn to participate in an experiment in which they were expected to receive painful electric shocks, were offered the opportunity to wait either alone or in the presence of others. It was observed that a significant proportion of the subjects preferred to wait in the presence of others faced with the same predicament. Now I'm not suggesting for one minute that you give your staff electric shocks if they don't maintain their takings every week, nor your clients if they don't turn up on time.

But there are times when the *concept* may be useful. For example, when interviewing for junior staff, it may put them more at ease if you seat applicants together in a waiting-room. Similarly, a new client may feel slightly anxious while waiting for her appointment, and although I'm not suggesting that you book all new clients together, the receptionist could certainly act as an agent to help reduce any anxiety by telling the client how competent your staff are.

Bystander apathy: what to do when things go wrong in the salon

In the early hours of an April morning in 1964, in Queens, New York, Catherine Genoase, returning home from her night job, was attacked and stabbed repeatedly over an extended period of time, until she was dead. Thirty-eight people, all of them residents of a respectable part of New York City, admitted to having witnessed at least part of the attack. But nobody went to her aid or called the police until after she was dead.

Perhaps you are as appalled as I am that a person should die without anybody making a move to help them, and again I am sure that you think, as I do, that had *you* witnessed such an incident you would have made some sort of effort to help. But have you never stood in a crowd, witnessed some sort of minor accident and although you wanted to help, for a split second you had been held back by a very powerful urge not to do anything? Maybe you would have felt that somebody more qualified than you will react, or you would not want to make a fool of yourself. Similarly, have you ever been present at the annual general meeting of your local hairdressing organisation when the call comes for nominations, or volunteers, to take on certain roles? Even though you might really fancy the job of chairman or public relations officer, etc., again you still hold back. Is it embarrassment or modesty? It doesn't matter, the same force that prevented action in Catherine Genoase's case has been working on you in exactly the same way. So, this force, this reluctance to intervene in situations that demand individual action from members of groups of people, is obviously very powerful. In 1968 two psychologists decided to

investigate this phenomenon and they set up a series of experiments to study 'bystander apathy' as they called it. In one of the studies a female experimenter asked one person to fill in a questionnaire, left him to it and went into another room.

Moments later, the subject heard her drag out a chair, climb onto it, fall over and scream. This experiment was repeated a number of times, the only variation being that fresh subjects were used and sometimes two people were asked to fill in questionaires instead of one. They found that the female experimenter was three-and-a-half times more likely to get aid if the subject was alone, than if there were two people in the room together.

In another ingenious set of experiments, subjects were asked to sit in a waiting-room while they waited to be called in to help with a simple experiment. As they were waiting, smoke slowly started to billow from underneath the connecting door. Again this experiment was repeated with only the number of subjects present being varied. With only one person present, the time it took from the appearance of smoke to their leaving the room was extremely short. With two people present, it took a lot longer before they left or even started to try and investigate the cause of the smoke. With three people in the room, some groups were still sitting there when the room was full of smoke with their eyes streaming. They gave all sorts of imaginary reasons for staying. None of them realised that it was only an experiment, they all perceived the situation as real, but most said things like, 'Nobody else moved, so I thought it must be alright.' This certainly mirrors the real-life situation and many store managers can tell stories of racing into the restaurant or cafeteria and instructing people to leave but most carried on calmly finishing their lunch.

Both these examples have direct parallels in the hairdressing salon. One is the situation where a client or member of staff faints or falls or has an accident and the other concerns a fire in the salon or the building it is situated in. There is a real danger that people will not act to save themselves. In the case of emergency aid (although in my opinion hairdressers are the sort of people who will act or speak up in a crowd) it is obvious that junior members of staff are more likely to be prone to the 'bystander apathy' syndrome.

In both cases, in order to avoid the likelihood of nobody becoming involved, perhaps it would be a good thing (1) to instruct members of staff in the theory of bystander apathy; and (2) to hold regular emergency drills so that the apathy is overridden by the response to the emergency which has become well learned due to practice.

Conclusion

What we have tried to show so far is that hairdressers practise human relations every working day, and that there are various methods of dealing with people, some of which may be more efficient than others. We have looked at how the brain functions and how memory is affected by the way information is fed to it and the amount and type of distractors there are. So the way you structure (1) the environment and (2) the information, can play an important part in efficient functioning. In trying to put a logical structure on creativity it was hoped to make it easier for you to view problems in different ways (to be more divergent in your approach). In particular we have tried to make you more aware of your own constraints (fear of failing, rigidity, etc.). We also thought it would be useful in the way you looked at concepts in this book and related them to real-life situations.

How you initially behave towards people is extremely important in developing a business based on personal relationships and the section on 'gain and loss of esteem' should have made you more aware of the potential consequences that spring from the initial attitude you adopt towards others.

With audience effects we have tried to show how important it is to *practise* any sort of skill that you wish to display to others and also how important it is to understand that the way you perceive the audience, for better or worse, can often have an effect on your performance.

Bystander apathy obviously relates to emergency situations in the salon, and knowing how damaging its effect may be can only lead to a greater feeling of security in your salon, by the knowledge that any situation can be dealt with more promptly.

Finally, I hope this chapter has given you a 'taste' of what 'psychology' is like, how it relates to your salon and how vital its application is in the running of a business. The next chapter deals with a subject which plays a crucial role in any hairdressing business—'first impressions'.

2. How Creating a Good Impression Can Improve Your Business

When questioned, most people say that they do *not* believe that they frequently judge people by their physical appearance. One of the aims of this chapter is to suggest that often, when meeting someone whom we do not know well, we *do* judge them by their appearance. This first impression they create influences our subsequent relationships with them. If they create a *good* first impression, then we do not immediately ignore them and this gives them an opportunity to show us their other qualities. However, if our first impression of them is poor, then we often ignore or do not listen to them and so they are deprived of the opportunity of showing us their possible true worth. First impressions are very important in the salon. What does the new client think of you, the salon and the staff when she first encounters them? Is the impression a good one? What do *you* think of a new client or someone coming for an interview when you first meet them? Are these judgements of use? What do they mean?

Why is it good to look attractive? Is it important to have attractive staff?

One reason why creating a good first impression is important is that much psychological research on attitude change has shown that if you wish to alter someone's opinion, this is much easier to do if they hold no views on the subject than when they hold views opposite to those you want them to have. What this means with regard to first impressions is that if a *poor* first impression is created, then it is very much more *difficult* to end up with the person or client thinking well of you or your services, than if initially a good first impression were created.

Psychologists are often accused of spending time finding out things that everybody already knows by common sense. There is some truth in this argument but it is important to find out whether what common sense suggests is really true. Psychologists carry out experiments in order to discover the truth, and in any business it is necessary to base decisions on facts. By means of their experiments they try to see what is fact and what is fiction about human behaviour. So, in this chapter we shall consider some of the facts about first impressions.

The appearance of your salon and staff plays a crucial role in the success of your business. *Perhaps almost as strong an influence as the hairstyles created.* You may doubt this, but studies of the effects of physical appearance strongly suggest that this is so.

"Madam, our new stylist, Sebastian, will do your hair for you."

One obvious person who can have an effect in this way is the receptionist, but the juniors, stylists and, in fact, the whole staff should strive to have appearances that fit in with your clients' expectations. Different salons and companies appeal to or attract different sorts of clients but the physical appearances of your staff should fit in with the image you wish to project.

This section will present evidence to show that when someone looks physically attractive, they are frequently more likely to reap the benefits that society can offer than someone who is 'unattractive' (or who has made themselves look unattractive because of their poor hair, make-up or clothing). This is important because it suggests first, that you should think about the effects that *your* appearance may have on other people; and second, that the hairdresser or beautician has a crucial role to play in enabling people to look their best.

A Canadian psychologist has argued that 'good-looking people are seen as possessing more sociably desirable traits and as having more future potential for happiness and success than unattractive individuals'. A similar observation was made by another psychologist, who asked people to give words to describe photographs of attractive and unattractive individuals. The attractive individuals were judged as more 'curious, complex, perceptive, academic, restless, confident, assertive, happy, active, amiable, humorous, pleasure-seeking, outspoken and flexible' than the unattractive individuals.

There are a number of ways of improving one's appearance, make-up and hair being obvious examples. Psychologists have confirmed the belief that attractiveness judgements are much higher for women when they are wearing make-up. Furthermore, in one experiment people's estimates of the hemline heights for women wearing make-up were noticeably higher than for women not wearing make-up when, in fact, all the women were wearing dresses with hems all the same height from the ground. Make-up was found to have a big effect on their judgement of the women as 'self-confident, sophisticated, snobbish' (with make-up), and as 'conventional, friendly, neat, religious' (without make-up). In this experiment when people were asked what they thought had influenced their impressions, none mentioned make-up.

This was also what happened in a study conducted over twenty years ago. Here six women were interviewed individually by a number of men, who were then required to fill in a form about each woman. In some interviews the women wore lipstick and in some they did not. This was found to have a strong effect on judgements of: frivolous—serious; talkative—introspective; anxious—placid; not conscientious—conscientious; marked—slight interest in the opposite sex (lipstick being

associated with the first of each pair). None of the male interviewers were reported as realising that lipstick was an important
feature in this study.

Other studies have noted that attractiveness ratings are low
for women wearing glasses. The wearing of glasses has been
found to influence judgements of intelligence. In one experiment, individuals rated the intelligence of women appearing on
film higher when the women wore glasses than when they did
not. This was so, at least, when the exposure was for fifteen
seconds. But when the exposure was for five minutes, during a
leisurely conversation, glasses had no effect on judgements of
intelligence.

Make-up is often used by women to boost their attractiveness; but what of men? Most men do not wear make-up, but
they can have beards. A psychologist showed sixty people a
picture of a bearded man, and another sixty one of the same
man clean-shaven. The observers were asked to write down their
opinions of this man. When bearded, the man was seen as more
enthusiastic, sincere, generous, extroverted, masculine, inquisi-
tive, strong and dirty.

Unfortunately few psychologists have ever experimentally
studied the effects of hairstyles or hair colour, and after you
have read this chapter you may well want to conduct an investi-
gation of your own. Why not?

Ten years ago in the United States a large number of people
were shown some pictures of male faces with different hair
length (crew cut, regular, or beatle cut), or hair colour (blonde,
black, or red), or amounts of scalp hair (regular, slightly balding, fairly bald), or hair quality (straight, wavy, curly), or facial
hair (clean-shaven, moustache or beard). They were asked to
judge each face plus hair for good—bad, kind—cruel, clean—
dirty, handsome—ugly, hard—soft, masculine—feminine,
large—small, virile—impotent, strong—weak, active—passive,
sharp—dull. It was found that when the faces had blonde hair
they were judged to be more kind than when the same faces had
black hair and the faces with black hair were judged as more
kind than those with red hair. Those with black hair were
judged to be the most 'active'. Those with 'regular' length hair
were judged to be 'bad' whereas when the same faces had crew
cuts they were judged to be clean, strong, virile, hard, masculine, active and sharp (one wonders whether this would have
been found in 1978, perhaps not). When the faces had beatle-
style hair, they were judged as good but dirty, and weak, soft,
impotent, feminine, inactive and dull! Faces with balding hair

were judged to be good and kind, but impotent, soft, weak and dull. Straight hair was rated as kind, good, clean, handsome, masculine, virile and strong, whereas curly hair was judged as bad, dirty, unkind, ugly, feminine, impotent and weak. The faces with moustaches were judged to be unkind, bad and hard, and those with beards were rated as dirty but also as strong and masculine. This rather simple study is the only one that psychologists have performed directly concerning the topic of hair. We can by no means be sure that people's judgements of faces and hair would really affect their behaviour, and also we cannot be sure that these views would hold today.

However, one topic which psychologists have studied extensively and which has a direct relationship to hairdressing and beauty is that of physical attractiveness. In many investigations attractive and unattractive experimenters have examined the reactions they get from the public, or the same experimenter has been made (via the use of hair and make-up) at one time to look attractive and then later to look unattractive and differences in people's behaviour towards the 'attractive' and 'unattractive' experimenter have been examined.

One theory is that attractive people develop greater self-confidence and so develop greater social skills. One consequence of this might be that unattractive people do not acquire the necessary social skills to make others want to get to know them when in fact they may have many things to offer. Psychologists have found a strong relationship between childhood social behaviour and later adult social adjustment, and since they have also shown that physically attractive children are the most popular with their classmates it is likely that they will become the more socially skilled adults. Here first impressions are important. It is much more difficult (and therefore many people do not bother) to get to know someone who is shy and lacks confidence. Thus, because people are nicer to attractive children, attractiveness comes to lead to the attractive children learning more social skills and then becoming better adjusted and more popular as adults.

One important reason why psychologists study physical attractiveness is for us to be aware of its operation. When this becomes so, then perhaps we will not favour those who by chance are the more attractive. Should this be the case then physically unattractive people will not suffer the rejection they frequently report. In only a few contexts does having a 'peculiar' face help (for example, being a comedian); in most it hinders and the hairdresser/beautician has an important job to do here.

One of the areas of behaviour in which most people would agree that physical attractiveness is important is that referred to by psychologists as 'dating and mating', and many people visit the salon so that their appearance may be enhanced (or transformed) before an important occasion. A great many studies have confirmed the fact that appearance is vitally important when a person goes to a social function, such as a party, and may have the desire to meet someone new with whom they can start up a dating relationship.

If one feels physically attractive then it is often true to say that one has more self-confidence, which may help to 'get off with' someone. It is also true that when a person is physically attractive they receive more pleasant approaches from other people and this boosts their self-confidence. In the 'dating' setting an individual's personality is also important, of course, but studies have shown that it is not as important as we might think and psychologists believe that an individual's personality can be moulded and affected by their own level of physical attractiveness.

Many studies and surveys of 'dating and courting' couples have shown that by far the most important factor to the partners at the beginning of the relationship was the other person's level of physical attractiveness. Most people have some idea of their own level of physical attractiveness (women having a more accurate self-opinion than do men) and psychologists have shown that we try to select as possible partners people of roughly the same level of attraction. Some men, of course, 'try for the moon' but they rarely succeed. If one takes photographs of courting or married couples, one photograph of one partner and a different photograph of the other partner and then one shows pictures of, say, thirty couples (sixty photographs in all, the photos being shuffled so that it is not clear who really partners whom) to people who do not know the couples, one finds that the attractiveness score given to a partner in a couple is very often highly similar to that given to the other partner. However, in some couples (but these are the minority) one of the partners is more attractive than the other.

Some other psychological studies have shown that the attractiveness of the more attractive partner 'rubs off' on the less attractive one. In one of these studies members of the public saw a man and a woman sitting side by side. Some people were told that the couple were married to each other and other people were not told anything about the relationship between the two people. The members of the public were asked to describe the kind of personality the man (who was of average attractiveness) would be likely to have. It was found that when the woman was attractive *and* supposedly married to the man, he was judged to have a nice, good personality. When she was made to look unattractive (by hair/make-up/clothing), if the man was thought to be married to her he was seen as having an unpleasant personality. Those members of the public who were not told that the couple were related judged the man as having an average personality whether or not the woman sitting next to him was attractive. This finding has implications for the salon. It seems as though attractiveness spreads from attractive people to their surroundings, and so it might well be true that if your staff (and the salon decor) are seen as attractive then the client's whole judgement of the service she has received may be more favourable than it otherwise might have been.

Studies of dating and friendship also show that sometimes *very high* physical attractiveness can put people off. We all know of the highly attractive person who believes that she is 'God's gift' and who is really rather bitchy. We avoid these people partly because we feel that they would not be interested in us anyway, and partly because their very high level of physical attractiveness has made life easy for them and 'underneath' their attraction they sometimes (but not always) have little to offer. This is an important point to bear in mind when selecting a receptionist for the salon. The receptionist should be reasonably attractive so that people warm to her and so that she is likely to have developed the social skills we shall now turn to, but she should not be *so* physically attractive that clients immediately think she might be bitchy.

Concerning social skills (the ability to talk, listen and converse well both verbally and non-verbally), there is now some evidence, though not as yet very much since few investigations have been on this topic, that physically attractive people do have more social skill than unattractive people. Tape recordings have been made, with permission, of people's telephone calls and then photographs taken of the participants. The conversations were judged by some people for the amount of social skill each person showed in the conversation and other people judged the talkers' photographs for physical attractiveness. A fairly strong relationship was found in that the more physically attractive a person's photograph was judged to be the more social skill they had. This finding has implications for staff who regularly interact with clients on the telephone, especially the receptionist. Again it seems that physically attractive people win out. If one is choosing a receptionist (or other staff), then all things being equal, one should choose the fairly attractive one since she is more likely to have more social skills – an ability very necessary when talking to clients.

We should now ask the question, why is it that the more physically attractive people have more social skill? Where does this relationship come from? People are not born with social skill, it is something which has to be learned and the most important time for this learning (as for most learning) is in childhood. Some learning of social skill can take place in adulthood and companies should ask themselves whether they might benefit from sending personnel on courses designed to enhance social skills.

In childhood psychologists believe, and many studies show, that the more attractive children (even as young as six years of age) are more popular with their classmates at school. Also the more physically attractive children usually create a more favourable impression on the teacher. Many studies have shown that when a piece of schoolwork is thought to have been written by an attractive person this receives more marks than if the same piece of work is thought to have been written by someone unattractive. This has implications for the job interview setting which is discussed in this book.

If it is true that the more attractive children have more friends and receive more favourable attention from their teachers, then we can see how they become more socially skilled. Because of the warm and positive approaches made to them they are, more so than the unattractive child, placed in situations in which they can learn and practise their social skills. One only has to think of the attractive teenager often being asked to social functions to see this in action. If the process described above does exist, and there is strong evidence that it does, then the hairdresser has a role to play when having children as clients.

Staying with the topic of the first impressions that children's appearance can create, it is clear from many psychological studies that physically unattractive children can be treated more harshly for the same misbehaviour than are attractive children. This has relevance to the salon when dealing with fellow staff or clients. Are you more or less pleasant, sympathetic, understanding, etc., with certain people than with others? If you have never thought about this, examine your own behaviour in the next few weeks to see if you are more pleasant to attractive than unattractive clients.

Who do you blame when things go wrong?

In a recent study in Canada, a number of children had two photographs taken, one of each child looking attractive (by the use of haircut/style and make-up) and the other photograph of the same child looking unattractive. Adults were asked to suggest what punishment they would give the child for certain misbehaviour and it was found that harsher punishment was suggested by those adults who saw the children in their unattractive state. Another study found that the attractiveness of the photograph on a schoolchild's report card had an effect upon judgements of misbehaviour. Women were given written details of a child's misbehaviour together with a photograph which was supposed to be of the child. The description of the misdeed was always exactly the same and the only thing that varied was that some people saw a photograph of an attractive child and some saw a photograph of an unattractive child. It was found that more lenient treatment was suggested for the attractive child. Those people who saw a photograph of an attractive child said that the misbehaviour was likely to be only a temporary thing whereas those with a photograph of an unattractive individual frequently said that they believed it more likely that the child was often naughty, was antisocial, and should be severely punished.

In a further study, experienced teachers were given a child's report card plus a photograph. The teachers were asked to say how likely it was that the child had been the naughty one in class and if so, what punishment should be given. As would be expected, the nature of the report card greatly influenced the teachers' decisions. If the report card was good then little punishment was suggested. However, if the report card was bad, the teachers who had the unattractive photograph were more inclined to suggest harsher punishment. We shall return to the topic of physical attractiveness and punishment later.

Another psychologist gave teachers a nursery schoolchild's report card to which was attached a photograph of the child. The teachers were asked to describe the child and it was found that although the report card always said exactly the same thing, the more attractive child in the photograph the more favourable were the teachers' descriptions of intelligence, popularity, likely future educational accomplishments, and parents' attitudes towards school. This finding is very similar to that found in the study mentioned at the very beginning of this section on first impressions, namely that attractive people are expected, by people who do not know them, to have nicer personalities. Do you have these same expectancies of clients and staff?

Some psychological studies have shown that the more attractive a person's face the more honest that person is judged to be. This sort of thing is strengthened by television, descriptions in books, etc. Casting directors of cinema and TV films frequently select actors to play parts for which they look 'right'. How many ugly people appear in TV advertisements? Very few. Two journalists in their study of films and novels found that villains tended to have dark and swarthy appearances whereas heroes tended to be blond.

Physical attractiveness is a variable which is currently receiving much attention from psychologists and research suggests that we might not expect people having certain appearances to be involved in crime. Recently two psychologists suggested that 'low physical attractiveness contributes to careers of deviancy' and a sociologist has noted that 'even social workers accustomed to dealing with all types often find it difficult to think of a normal, pretty girl as being guilty of a crime. Most people, for some inexplicable reason, think of crime in terms of abnormality of appearance and I must say that beautiful women are not often convicted.' It has already been mentioned that film and advertising directors have for years chosen as the 'baddy' a small, ugly, weasel-looking individual and as the 'goody' a tall, attractive, clean-cut type.

In one experiment in which people were asked to behave exactly as they would do in a real court-room, and in which they heard a court case and then acted as the jury, it was found that the attractiveness of the person being accused of the crime had an effect on how many years' imprisonment the jurors suggested the judge should give. When found guilty of burglary the jurors who saw an attractive woman as the accused person suggested about six years but other jurors who heard exactly the same case but for whom the accused looked unattractive (her hair and make-up were poor) suggested nine years' imprisonment (three years more). So here again being attractive seems to help. However, other jurors who heard a swindling case in which the woman persuaded a man to part with his money, were displeased by the woman using her beauty in unfair ways.

Those who saw the attractive swindler suggested *more* years' imprisonment than those who saw the unattractive swindler. So it doesn't always pay to be attractive!

"I know one of you has been booking phantom clients".

Some psychologists in Aberdeen have been studying the 'photofit' system that witnesses use to reconstruct for the police a face they have seen. (You may have seen some of these on 'Police Five' or on the TV news.) In this study all the reconstructors (housewives) were shown the same face but half of them were told it was the face of a murderer, whereas the other half were told that it was of a lifeboat-man. The face was removed and the women were asked to construct a photofit of it. When this had been done they were asked to describe the original face. The next stage of this study involved presenting the photofit faces constructed by the housewives to a new group of women who were required to describe the faces. It was found that the photofits of the face said to be of a lifeboat-man were judged to be much more attractive and intelligent than the photofits of the same face when it was described as being that of a murderer.

When interviewing someone, can first impressions lead you to make a wrong decision?

If you are involved in interviewing applicants for a job in the salon, are you affected by their appearance? Might you also be influenced by the way they have filled in the application form? On many occasions when more than just a few applicants apply for a post, only some of these will be called to interview, this selection being performed on the basis of the job application form (which may be in the applicant's own handwriting with a photograph attached).

It is a common observation that good handwriting enables one easily to tell what the writer is trying to say whereas poor handwriting makes reading rather more difficult. Some studies have found that teachers can give higher grades to an essay written in good handwriting than when the same essay is written in poor handwriting.

These studies of physical attractiveness do suggest that this factor can have a very widespread influence, so the hairdresser can help people to look attractive while at the same time being aware of how first impressions are important in the client/staff relationship and in the interview setting.

Three years ago some German psychologists examined the importance of applicants' sex, physical attractiveness and scholastic achievement in the evaluation of job applications. Thirty experienced personnel interviewers and thirty students studying industrial management each received twelve completed application forms (plus photographs of the applicants) for the post of the head of a section in a large department store. The psychologists varied these applications in terms of the sex, scholastic achievement and physical attractiveness of the applicant. The assessors were asked to evaluate each of the applications and it was found that scholastic achievement, physical attractiveness and sex of applicant each had a strong effect on judged suitability for the post. This was the case both for the experienced personnel interviewers and for the students. We should note that these findings may have been caused by the job description which specified 'a high degree of interpersonal skill', the very thing needed in hairdressing.

A similar experiment was conducted by another psychologist. Here eighty personnel managers each assessed one application for a post in a personnel department. The applications varied in the sex, physical attractiveness and qualifications of the applicant, and the assessors were required to indicate whether they would recommend employment. They were also required to evaluate the applicant's personality. For the decisions concerning employment recommendation *both* the factors of qualifications and physical attractiveness had strong effects, and the

"She's very attractive, but she has poor references. Never mind, she'll be good for the salon and so I'll give her the job."

attractiveness of the applicant influenced how much the personnel managers thought they would like the applicant and how hard-working the applicant would be. This study again demonstrates that the physical attractiveness of the photograph on a job application form can influence employment decisions and this effect is also likely to occur when you are face to face with someone.

Does your appearance matter when you are giving advice?

If you are a manager and sometimes a member of your staff wants to discuss something personal with you or you want to question them, studies of therapy situations where a person seeks advice have shown that the appearance of the therapist (manager?) can be important. In a recent experiment, people were shown a film of someone giving advice individually to some students concerning personal problems they had been

Manager: "You need to smarten up your appearance!"

experiencing. Some people saw the counsellor with his usual (attractive) appearance and others saw him in an unattractive condition in which he was made to look much fatter, had bags under his eyes and his hair was 'less stylishly groomed'. The advice he gave and the way he presented it was identical in both his attractive and unattractive appearances. Those people who saw him with the attractive appearance judged him to be a more likeable, warm, competent, trustworthy, assertive, friendly and intelligent counsellor or adviser than those people who saw him with his unattractive appearance. Other people who listened just to tape recordings of the advice sessions did not differ in their judgements of the counsellor whether the tape recordings were made in the attractive or unattractive appearance state. Therefore, it was simply the counsellor's appearance which influenced the judgements of his ability. This is important because if you are going to advise someone then they are more likely to take your advice if you appear competent, trustworthy, warm, etc. Also, of course, do not be fooled by someone who simply dresses to appear 'right' when in fact, underneath, they do not have the qualities that their appearance suggests.

What are the effects of the way you look at people and of the clothing you wear?

All these studies illustrate how we often do judge people by their appearance, and that these judgements which we make go on to force us to make other (often wrong) conclusions about them. We have just seen that the nature of the crime is important when deciding whether the culprit's physical attractiveness will be of benefit to them or not.

Getting a good look at people is important for all sorts of reasons and chapter 3 discusses this point. There does seem to be some truth in the idea that people who look you in the eye when answering your questions are more likely to be believed by you.

In one study a female student went round knocking on people's front doors asking for money to be donated to a children's charity. When someone answered the door she either looked them straight in the eyes during the first five seconds when asking for money, or she did not look them in the eyes at all, but looked at the collecting tin when asking for money. Thus half the people opening their front doors received the non-verbal communication of eye contact and the other half did not. It was found that more people gave more money when the charity collector looked them in the eyes than when she did not, and the effect of this factor was even more pronounced when the collector was dressed casually in jeans and a teeshirt. On half the occasions when she was collecting money the collector was dressed in a smart two-piece suit. When this was worn more money was given in the eye-contact condition than in the no eye-contact condition. However, the effect of eye contact was extremely pronounced in the casual dress condition. It is as if the members of the public did not react very favourably to the casual dress, but if when so attired the collector looked them in the eyes, this made a good first impression.

We shall now briefly examine some studies of the effect of clothing. This is not so relevant to hairdressers as those studies in which hairstyle and make-up have been used to create an impression of attractiveness or unattractiveness, but the message is the same.

Most of the body is hidden by clothes, consequently the clothes themselves are a major element in appearance and can therefore be thought of as playing an important part in impression formation. Like hair, clothes can be clearly distinguished at a distance, whereas facial features and tone of voice require closer inspection. In a society in which brief social contacts are numerous, clothing has become an important index of behaviour and status. Impressions based on facial expression, gestures, physique and style of dress are widely accepted. Judgements of others' clothes are so much a part of our social experience that we tend to overlook their significance in the analysis of social behaviour. A few years ago a psychologist arranged for some women's personalities to be described when they were wearing different sorts of clothing. It was found that the women were given different social status and personality ratings, depending on the clothing they wore. Previously, there had been a similar reaction when photographs of the same men in different clothes were used. Recently it was found that personality judgements of women by a class of students were similar on two occasions, three weeks apart, when the same clothes were worn on both occasions by some of the women. But they were not similar for the women who wore different clothes on the second occasion.

In another experiment, fifty people judged photographs of women wearing different dresses. The people were found to agree on which women appeared to be 'sophisticated, conventional, intelligent, religious, imaginative'. When only the faces from the photographs were rated, there was no agreement at all. Dresses, therefore, can have pronounced effects on such impressions. Another psychologist took photographs of four male and four female students in four different kinds of dress (school uniform, casual, working, evening). Thirty men and thirty women then judged these photographs for features such as pleasant, youthful, interesting, good. That clothing had an effect was evident from the marked tendency for the judgement to be low when a person wore school uniform and high when the same person wore evening dress.

Style of dress has an effect in those situations where one individual asks for help from another. In one study the experimenters approached various individuals and asked for the money to make a telephone call. The male and female experimenters were dressed either smartly or casually and it was found that more of those wearing casual dress received money. Surprisingly, it was found that the male experimenters often got more help than the female. But since this experiment took place on a university campus it may not be possible to generalise these findings to the high street.

In almost all of the studies mentioned so far, the smart or attractive individual has received the better treatment. But what is meant by 'smart' and 'attractive'? After all, what is attractive to one person may not be so to another. Most of the studies concerned with this found that observers *agreed* about which faces were physically attractive. There is usually agreement about clothing too, but a study of petition-signing draws attention to the importance of the type of individuals used as subjects in these experiments. During a peace demonstration experimenters asked for signatures for an anti-war petition. The experimenter who was dressed scruffily obtained more agreements to sign from the demonstrators than the one who was smartly dressed. Another psychologist noticed a similar result if a person wore a tie. Here individuals were approached and asked whether they would give their addresses so that a travel survey could be sent to them. One group of subjects were those entering a Conservative club and another those entering a transport cafe. Men entering the Conservative club were more willing to give their addresses when the experimenter was wearing a tie than when he was not. Those entering the transport cafe were not influenced by whether the experimenter was or was not wearing his tie.

As far as honesty is concerned, an American psychologist found that when individuals in telephone booths were asked to return a dime which the experimenter had left in the booth, 77 per cent of the individuals returned the dime when the experimenter was dressed smartly and only 30 per cent did so when dressed casually. In Texas, it was observed that more pedestrians violated a compulsory 'don't cross' sign at a road crossing when a smartly dressed experimenter did so than when a poorly dressed one did. In London experiments have been carried out which showed that more individuals were prepared to answer some market research questions when the questioners were dressed smartly than when they were dressed casually.

Conclusion

Physical appearance is often believed to affect a person's opinion change, an important factor in many settings, including the court-room. Individuals who appear in advertisements are very often physically attractive, and this is not just to catch the observer's attention. It has been demonstrated experimentally that a physically attractive communicator is more persuasive than an unattractive one, even when it was made clear that the intention was specifically to produce a change of attitude.

All these results from a great many studies are most important with regard to the hairdressing profession because they suggest that members of the public are more inclined to react favourably to someone who, to them, has a pleasing appearance.

You may not believe that this is so. Many psychologists were very sceptical about the effects of physical appearance when they first started conducting research in this area, *but now it seems true that physical appearance can have profound effects on behaviour:* and where is the one place in which members of the public would expect pleasing physical appearances to abound? *Why, in hair and beauty salons, of course!* Think about it!

3. Impression Management in the Salon

Introduction

One of the major features which distinguishes humans from the rest of the animal kingdom is self-awareness. Each of us is conscious of ourselves and we are all capable of reflecting on our own actions in a way which is uniquely human. Now, the implications for social behaviour of this human characteristic are truly enormous; and, in this chapter, we shall explore some of them for the rather special social world of hairdressing.

To the social psychologist, hairdressing is an unusual and interesting profession in so far as it is concerned with the social reconstruction of other people's selves. As a hairdresser, your role in society is to support and enhance the kind of self which each individual wants to present to the rest of the world. Your business is primarily one of helping to maintain, and often reconstruct, a person's self-image.

If you accept this social psychological view of hairdressing, then it follows that the kind of relationship you have with your client will be of critical importance to the success of your business. Hairdressing is far more than the application of a set of *manipulative* skills, acquired during apprenticeship, together with whatever dash of creativity you are fortunate enough to possess. It involves a range of *social* skills which go far beyond expertise and creativity in fashioning hair.

In this respect, then, the relationship between you and your client is like that between doctor and patient. This is not as far-fetched as it may at first seem. There is considerable evidence to show that doctors who are most successful in curing their patients are those who possess, and are competent in exercising, a range of personal and social skills over and above their specialised medical knowledge. Such doctors are said to have a 'good bedside manner'.

47

Now it is likely that it is those hairdressers who implicitly recognise this social element in their profession, and who conduct their business both *in* and *with* the right manner, who are most successful in attracting and retaining clients. Similarly, when a salon manager is unable to hold on to clientele — despite evidence of the high quality of actual hairdressing carried out — it may well have something to do with the social climate of the salon.

In this chapter, you may find that we simply spell out much of what you already do — though you may not always know clearly why you do it. Social skills are in this respect rather like musical skills. Some people can play the piano without being able to read a note of music. Similarly, some salon managers — though by no means all — show very considerable social skills in the salon without ever having read any psychology.

To know *why* things happen rather than simply knowing *that* they happen, of course, won't make much difference when your business is prospering. However, it can make all the difference between success and closure when turn-over begins to falter or a crisis blows up. So, in this chapter, we shall help you to read the music of your salon and to identify some of the major themes underlying the business of hairdressing. With this knowledge, you will be in a better position to control what happens and when it happens in your salon.

What is the 'looking-glass self'?

According to social psychologists, whose job it is to study human social behaviour, one of the most interesting things about human beings is the way in which the self-image of each of us is dependent on other people's evaluations of us. For a great deal of the time, what we do and how we do it is affected by our anticipation of how others will react to our behaviour. It's almost as if we carry round with us, inside our heads, voices of approval and disapproval which influence how we behave.

Let us consider one or two examples. Think of the last occasion when you planned to take something that didn't belong to you; perhaps a cigarette from a colleague's packet or a sweet from your daughter's 'secret' hoard in her toy cupboard. The momentary feeling of shame or guilt which you experienced at that moment was but one example of the way we anticipate other people's reactions to us.

Or, think of the last occasion when you found yourself in an embarrassing situation. I'm sure that a moment's reflection will tell you that your embarrassment consisted precisely of the anticipated reactions of other people to your predicament. Of course, I have given rather dramatic illustrations of the influence which others have on us inside our heads. It is an influence which is very pervasive. It largely determines how we see ourselves, whether we evaluate ourselves positively or negatively, and in turn, how we respond to other people.

How is this so? To answer this question, we need to understand how a person comes to acquire a sense of self in the first place. We are not born with a sense of self. It is something which we acquire or which emerges as we grow out of infancy. Initially, the new-born infant simply reacts to *internal feelings,* such as pangs of hunger or stomach-ache due to wind, or to *external stimulation* such as being touched by its mother or chafed by wet nappies, which produce pleasure or discomfort. At this stage, it is no more conscious of itself than a cat or dog can be said to be conscious of itself. But, gradually, through a process of interaction with others, the young infant will begin to become aware of itself as a separate being. It will slowly become aware of itself as an object to other people, that is, it realises that others, usually its parents and brothers and sisters, are reacting to it.

So, these reactions of others to you as a growing child make you feel loved or unloved; they tell you whether you are good or naughty, clever or stupid, pretty or plain, and a thousand and one other things about yourself. This goes on day after day throughout you early childhood. And what happens is that you *internalise* these reactions and evaluations of yourself by others. You make them your own reaction and evaluation of yourself. In other words, they become *your* self-image.

Thus you end up acquiring a self which is a composite of all the reactions of others towards you which you have experienced since the day you were born. The image that you have of yourself is simply the reflection of how others see you. You take on the attitudes, reactions and evaluations of other people towards you as *your own* attitude, reaction and evaluation of yourself.

A famous sociologist once coined the phrase 'the looking-glass self' to describe this process whereby each of us comes to know who and what we are by realising how others see us. Just as you look at your reflection in a mirror to see what you look like, so, in much the same way, you see who and what you are by seeing yourself reflected in other people's reactions to you.

We can now begin to see, therefore, how it is that other people can influence our self-image and why it is that we are continuously sensitive to their evaluations of us. As you grow up and come into contact with wider sections of society, your childhood self will undergo changes. You will come to occupy an increasing number of positions or roles in society — for example, as manager of a hairdressing salon, as spouse or lover, as parent, as member of a social club, and so forth. And each of these social roles will have an impact on your sense of self. You will increasingly see yourself in terms of these social roles. Thus, for example, being an hairdresser will be an important part of your self-image.

Now, in so far as there are expectations as to how you should behave attached to every role, then your self-image will be largely shaped by the degree to which you meet these expectations successfully or otherwise. The part of yourself which is invested in hairdressing will feel good in so far as you are a good hairdresser. And whatever part of you is invested in being a parent will feel good in the degree to which you meet the expectations which society has of how a parent should be. But how do you know whether you are a good hairdresser or a good parent? You know primarily by a process of social comparison. That is, you compare yourself with other hairdressers and with other parents. And the major way in which you do this is by responding implicitly to their reactions to you. You respond to the countless cues which they give out and which communicate to you whether or not they hold you in high regard. You are all the time looking for information which will tell you what kind of person you are. In some sense then, your self is not your own possession — it's on loan from society. If society's evaluation of you should change, then your evaluation of yourself will surely change.

How to create a good impression

However, we are not totally passive with respect to other people's evaluations of us. There is a definite sense in which we can be said to be actively engaged in impression management. Throughout any social encounter we seek to present ourselves in such a way to others that their reactions to us confirm the image of ourselves which we wish to hold. We adopt a particular front or face and use a variety of strategies to support it. Embarrassment or loss of face occurs when for some reason events overtake us and the image which we are presenting is disconfirmed. Or to put it another way, loss of face is a result of impression *mis*management.

The hairdressing salon is particularly interesting in this respect, because clients present a self in the salon which they don't normally present in public. Physical appearance is one of the major ways in which we communicate to others who we are. Clothing, hairstyle and make-up are all vehicles for impression management. Most people do not like to be caught unawares by unexpected visitors, because the self we have at home is different from the self we present to the outside world. Think how often a woman caught unexpectedly by visitors will slip quickly into another room to brush her hair and put on some make-up. We talk about making ourselves 'presentable'. Now, in the salon, just in order to be able to build a new public self, a client must risk presenting a self without the usual props. The hairdresser is contracted to build this new self out of the tarnished one which enters the salon.

Many hairdressers report that they do not mix socially with their clients and will actually avoid contact if an opportunity occurs, for example, through a chance encounter in a pub or restaurant. In so doing, they are responding to the special nature of the relationship which they have with their clients. As a hairdresser, you have seen your clients presenting a very different self in the salon to the one which you now see them presenting in public. Your client will feel somewhat uneasy, therefore, at this reminder of a different self from the one which she is now presenting. She will not be pleased to encounter you; you are an intrusion from another social world. In this respect, hairdressers have much in common with doctors, who also have privileged access to aspects of a person's self, which are not normally open to public scrutiny.

Social interaction as a performance

Given then that we have a number of selves or sub-selves which belong to the various social roles which we occupy and given that in each of these social roles we strive to present a self which is consonant with the role, we can now see that every social encounter is a performance. It is a performance in which each of the interactants collaborates to support the particular self which each of them is presenting. All social interaction therefore is not only a performance but also a collaboration. Thus, in the context of the hairdressing salon, you and your staff can be regarded as engaged in a collaborative performance. If you doubt this analysis, then simply consider the kind of behaviour which you engage in when clients are present in the salon and the rather different behaviour after the last one has gone at closing time or backstage where the coffee is made. I'm sure that it differs markedly. Alternatively, think whether your manner would change if a close friend came into your salon.

Some people seem to get rather upset when it is pointed out to them that all social interaction is a performance. They somehow feel that this implies that they are insincere. However, this is rarely the case. Probably the con-man is the only totally cynical social performer. Most of us are completely sincere in the performance which we are engaged in. However, being sincere does not mean that your behaviour is not a performance.

The self-image of the client

So far we have been rather theoretical. This was necessary in order to introduce you to concepts and ideas which will enable you to look at your profession in a new way. We shall now turn to what actually happens in the salon when a woman comes to have her hair done.

There are certainly a great many different reasons why a woman wants her hair done. For many women we can probably quickly compile a list of social engagements, such as dinner parties, weddings, trips to the theatre and so forth. In all such cases, she will be wanting to present herself as well groomed and attractive as possible. In other words, she will be wanting to enhance her self-image for a specific social event. However, on many other occasions women come to the salon when there is no immediate social engagement and in a good many cases, I suspect, they come when they are feeling unloved and depressed. Many hairdressers will know of clients of their own who come to them when they seem low or depressed and who, when they leave the salon, are often much happier and more confident. Therefore, having one's hair done is one important way of changing one's total feelings about oneself. The successful hairdresser is the one who is sensitive to the feelings or mood state of his clients and who is able to transform both their appearance *and* their feelings.

Let us look at this a little more closely. When a woman has visited the salon, her friends will tell her how attractive she looks. And she in turn, because she feels attractive with her new hairstyle, will carry herself better. She feels more confident and the image that she *does* present is more confident as well. In other words, her confidence in her new hairstyle will largely determine the kind of image she does present. If she is not confident, then she will carry herself badly and her friends will not give her the kind of reinforcement she wants. As her hairdresser you have created a new hairstyle for her, but it doesn't follow automatically that you have created a new image for her. What has to happen is that she must be convinced *by you and your staff* that the style you've created for her is totally successful. She has got to believe that she will be admired when she returns to her friends and contacts outside the salon. She must feel right when she leaves the salon. She must feel confident in herself. Now, if she does feel right, if she does feel confident when she leaves the salon, then it's more likely that she *will* receive

the admiration and confirmation of her self-image from her friends and contacts. It will be her very confidence in herself which will largely influence their reaction to her. And if she is successful, then she is likely to return to your salon on future occasions. Conversely, of course, if she doesn't feel right, if she lacks the necessary confidence in herself, then she will almost certainly carry herself in such a way that admiration and confirmation of her new image will not be forthcoming. She will doubt her own attractiveness and these doubts will be picked up and reflected back to her by others. If this occurs, it is unlikely that she will visit your salon again.

So, what mainly determines whether or not a woman feels right is not so much the actual hairdressing but rather the total message which she picks up from the many cues which you and your staff give out and which indicate whether or not you are competent, caring and pleased with your creation. In fact, from the moment that she enters the salon, she will be seeking reassurance that the decision she has taken to come to you has been the right one. Of course, a good salon will constantly provide this reassurance. This can be done both at the verbal and at the non-verbal level. To give an example, when the treatment is finished, your stylist should tell her how good she looks, even calling over a junior to show him/her the creation. Your receptionist should also admire her hair when she pays the bill. And you as manager, if you are available when she is leaving the salon, should also reinforce her confidence in the new image which you have created for her. Details like this may seem trivial and time-wasting to you and to your staff, but they may well be crucial to your business, since they influence whether or not your clients come back again.

However, much of the information which a client picks up is given off non-verbally and is summed up in what I have earlier called 'manner'. It is the manner of your receptionist, your juniors, your stylist and yourself which will create the climate of the salon. It is this climate which will make the client feel that she is salient or insignificant, secure or insecure, confident or anxious. Every client should feel that she is receiving the best possible attention in the best possible salon. She needs to be made to feel important because, for her, having her hair done is critically important. She is entrusting her self-image to another person. She is making herself very vulnerable and she needs desperately to feel that the treatment she gets will be the best for her. She must be made to feel that she is the most important client that the hairdresser has, just as a patient needs to feel that she has all the doctor's care and attention.

Now, one of the problems connected with non-verbal communication or manner is that we are often largely unaware of the impression we create until someone points this out to us. The non-verbal behaviour which we give out is often unintentional but no less powerful in its impact on others. Therefore you and your staff may be largely unaware of the cues you are giving out. But you can be equally certain that your client is picking them up. She wouldn't necessarily be able to articulate what it is she is reacting to but might simply remark that she didn't like the salon and wouldn't be going there again. She will have reacted to all the cues which tell her what kind of person you think she is, what kind of treatment you are giving her and what kind of image you have created for her. She will be picking up information all the time — from the moment she first telephones or calls in to make an appointment, to the moment when she finally leaves the salon having paid the bill.

The Anatomy of Manner

During the past fifteen years or so social psychologists have discovered a great deal about the many components of manner or non-verbal communication. A major outcome of their research has been the setting-up of training centres for people who are hopelessly inept in their social skills. It would seem that most of us manage to acquire the elements of non-verbal communication during our childhood and these enable us to get by more or less successfully in our everyday social encounters. However, for some reason there are a few people who fail to acquire these communicative skills and, because they constantly give out the wrong cues in social interaction, soon end up socially isolated and shunned by other people. At a less extreme level, it is obvious that most people are variously successful in conducting their interactions with others. It is probably the case that those individuals who are popular and well liked are the ones who have most successfully acquired a repertoire of social skills which they then apply appropriately in each new social encounter.

What we want to do in this chapter is to describe some of the findings of this research with a view to alerting you to their implications for your salon. Ideally, we should do this by presenting back to you on video-tape your own non-verbal behaviour. From experience on our residential courses, we have found this to be the most effective way of tuning hairdressers into the importance of manner in the business of hairdressing. Therefore in discussing the separate components of non-verbal communication it is important to keep in mind that they are separate only for the purpose of this analysis and that in reality they are all part of a single behavioural flow.

Eye contact

One of the most important as well as most researched aspects of manner is eye contact, that is, the amount and quality of looking or gazing at another person. It is one of the major vehicles for signalling a whole host of information to another person. We use it to indicate to someone that we are attracted to them, as for example, when you catch and hold someone's gaze for just a fraction longer than normal at a party. We use it to indicate friendliness, interest and appreciation as well as to give reassurance and reduce anxiety. It is a sign of frankness and openness and we tend to mistrust a person who avoids eye contact. Thus, a person who avoids eye contact simply out of a crippling shyness may come to be avoided by other people who misinterpret this avoidance as an indication of deviousness. Such a person would clearly benefit from the kind of social skill training we described above.

Some aspects of eye contact are not really under our control as, for example, with pupil dilation. It has been found that when we look at someone or something which we find attractive or desirable, the pupils of our eyes dilate. And in turn we respond unconsciously to the size of people's pupils. For example, in one psychological experiment it was found that

"Now look at the eyes on the front cover"

when presented with pairs of identical photographs of girls' faces and asked to choose the one they preferred, men consistently chose the photo in which the pupils were larger. In other words, the photos were not completely identical but differed in the size of the pupils. However, when asked why they had chosen a particular photograph, the men were unable to give a reason. They were unaware that they had been affected by the size of the girls' pupils. Although it is only recently that psychologists have discovered the importance of pupil size, it is interesting that this was known to be important in sexual attraction in the Middle Ages, when women put belladonna in their eyes to enlarge the pupils.

Other aspects of eye contact, however, *are* within our control and in this respect are of importance in the salon. Research has shown that there is a definite pattern of gaze and mutual gaze during any conversation and that its function is to regulate who speaks and who listens. Thus, for example, as person *A* comes to the end of what they want to say, they will look at person *B* (the listener) and continue looking for a short while as person *B* begins to speak. However, person *B* actually looks away as they begin to speak. If this pattern of gaze and mutual gaze does not occur, then person *B* (the listener) is likely to delay speaking or will not respond at all. So, what we find is that a speaker will look at the listener to indicate that they have finished what they want to say or to seek permission to continue. They will look away from the listener at the beginning of speaking and whenever they have to think carefully what they want to say. One of the noticeable features of the bore is that he avoids eye contact with you when button-holing you; he does this in order to avoid having to seek permission with his eyes to continue speaking. In so doing he inhibits you from interrupting without great difficulty. Of course, this is to impute a degree of conscious manipulation of others to him of which the bore may be totally unaware. He may be another example of a suitable case for social skill training. Indeed, we are almost totally unaware of the pattern of eye contact which we engage in during a conversation. It is something we learn implicitly and without training during our early childhood. Nevertheless, its impact is enormous and in the degree to which we become aware of our own patterns of gaze, the greater will be our control over any social encounter.

One of the reasons why many people find telephone conversations difficult may well be because they are normally very dependent on eye contact with the person they are talking to. In a series of experiments conducted in Oxford, it was found that most people reported that they felt uncomfortable when they were asked to conduct conversations with other people either when blindfold or from behind a screen. We do seem to rely fairly heavily on eye contact with others. If we are deprived of this for some reason, then we feel unhappy about the interaction.

How is this relevant to the salon? There are at least three areas which come immediately to mind. You may be able to think of several more. First, many hairdressers engage their clients in conversation while attending to their hair. There are probably quite large individual differences and the good hairdresser will be sensitive to the feelings of his/her client. Some clients want to talk, others don't. But, in many cases, a hairdresser will encourage self-disclosure on the part of the client, in order to get to know what she is like. The better he/she knows the client, the easier it is to find the right style or cut for her. A good hairdresser matches the cut to the whole person. Our personalities animate our bodies, so by talking to the client the hairdresser hopes to draw out her personality. Now, if she looks only at her head while talking to her, this may impede the conversation or even make her feel uncomfortable. She will not be able to relax sufficiently to talk about herself. It would seem sensible, therefore, for a hairdresser to engage in fairly frequent eye contact with the client while talking to her. And to do this, of course, the mirror can be used. It might be argued, however, that by frequently looking up from the work to maintain eye contact with the client, the treatment will take longer and thus be more expensive to the salon. But surely, if the outcome of this change is to make the client feel more relaxed and to increase the likelihood that she will return, it will be well worth it. And anyway, we are talking about eye contact that on each occasion lasts no more than a second or two.

The second area where eye contact is important is at the reception desk. Your receptionist is your front line — the first person whom your client encounters when she enters the salon. So, presumably the kind of reception a client receives is going to be crucial to everything which happens subsequently. The receptionist sets the tone of your establishment and predisposes the client to react favourably or otherwise to the treatment she subsequently receives. The first impression is at reception. This makes it a critical area for the success of your business. Now, many receptionists unwittingly curtail their eye contact with clients. This happens largely because they tend to be working with an appointments book and to be sitting lower down than the client. The natural tendency is not to look up except at the beginning of the encounter with a client. However, from what we now know about the importance of eye contact in making people feel attractive and comfortable, it is clearly essential that your receptionist is encouraged to maintain regular eye contact with clients.

Furthermore, a receptionist should also look squarely at the

client when handing her the bill. Receptionists frequently tend to avoid eye contact at this critical moment. Yet, since eye contact is a primary indicator of openness, it makes good sense for the client to receive her bill in as open a manner as possible.

Finally, since people differ in the degree to which they engage in eye contact, you cannot take it for granted that all your staff maintain an optimum level with clients. It seems worth while, therefore, informing your staff of the importance of this dimension of non-verbal communication. Whatever the norm of each member of staff may be, the fact of being made aware of the importance of eye contact creates the possibility of change. Needless to say this must be done gently and tactfully by a manager.

Smiling

Closely tied in with the pattern of eye contact is facial expression and, in particular, smiling. We find it very difficult not to be influenced by someone's smile. It is difficult to resist and almost inevitably makes us feel good. This is probably because there is an innate mechanism in all of us which responds automatically to a smile. We know, for instance, from studies of new-born infants that we do not learn to respond to a smile — it is already coded in us from birth. Babies will respond almost from birth to a smiling face and do so much more readily than to a non-smiling face.

Since receiving a smile is such a very powerful signal from someone, it is likely to be absolutely critical in the salon. First, because it will be a major indicator of the attitude of yourself and your staff to your client. It signals to her that she is in a warm, friendly and safe environment; and it also tells her that she is welcome. It will make her feel likeable and attractive and will certainly help her to relax in a situation where she is likely to feel tense and anxious. A smiling welcome and a smiling good-bye from the receptionist may well be a critical factor in determining the success of a client's visit to your salon. As a manager, you must ask yourself whether your salon seems a friendly place. Do your staff smile at clients? Do they indeed smile at each other? If they don't, then sure enough there is something wrong with your salon and your clients will sense this. If the atmosphere is cold, then the client will not feel comfortable. If she does not feel comfortable, she is unlikely to return.

A second reason for paying attention to smiling in your salon is that it can be a very useful barometer of the state of your clients. A person will often smile to cover anxiety or even fear.

Your staff need to be sensitive to the quality of smiles which they receive from clients. This becomes important when discussing treatment with a client. She will not want to be pressurised but may be too overawed or anxious to disagree or refuse. It is therefore important to monitor her smiles. Do they indicate nervousness or is she relaxed? And at the same time be aware of her head nods and head shakes. Normally, we nod our heads in conversation to signal agreement and to keep the conversation going. And conversely, we shake our heads to indicate disagreement. However, when someone is tense or anxious, they can betray their feelings by head nods and shakes. Thus, if you ask a client whether she wants a particularly expensive treatment, she may say yes, while at the same time slightly shaking her head. This may well be an unconscious signal that she doesn't want it at all but is too timid to say so. A client who allows herself to be pressurised into something she doesn't want, is unlikely to return to your salon on a future occasion. A hard sell will in all probability be your last sell to that client. Therefore it is wise policy to be sensitive to the cues which your clients give out.

Tone of voice

Another major indicator of warmth and friendliness is tone of voice. It is amazing just how unaware most people are of how they sound to others, until they hear a recording of their voice. Again, this aspect of manner is critical to the successful running of your salon, and, most especially, at reception. Whenever appointments are made over the telephone, eye contact and facial expression are automatically ruled out. The very first impression that a client will form of your establishment will be largely shaped by your receptionist's manner on the telephone.

When a client first picks up the phone and contacts your salon to make an appointment, she must be made to feel important. She will need to feel that the salon will look after her and give her the best possible service. The impression of the salon which she gets from talking to the receptionist will be conveyed as much by how she speaks to her as by what she says. There is all the difference in the world between 'I'm sorry, I can't fit you in at this particular time. We're extremely busy', said in a neutral voice; and 'I'm sorry, I can't fit you in at *this* particular time. I'm afraid we're very busy at present. But I'll certainly see what I can do for you', said in a friendly tone of voice. In the first case, the client will feel unimportant and unwanted; in the second, she will immediately feel that this is a salon which makes an effort for clients and cares for their welfare.

Or, to give another example: a potential client phones the salon and says 'Hello'. Now, the receptionist might simply reply, 'This is X's Salon' and leave it to the client to then say what she wants. Alternatively, the receptionist might say, 'Good morning. This is X's Salon. *Can I help you?*' in a friendly voice. Obviously these are two very different approaches. The second clearly indicates to the client that the receptionist is not out simply to sell an appointment but is going to help her. If a receptionist looks on her job as one of helping a client to achieve the best solution to the mutual benefit of client and salon, then this positive attitude will certainly come across to clients. It will largely be conveyed by her tone of voice. This will be a pleasure to clients and will be an important influence in determining whether or not a client comes back again. It would seem vital therefore, when interviewing applicants for a job in your salon as receptionist, to choose someone who has a warm and friendly voice.

Touch

Hairdressers, like doctors and nurses, are in an interesting position with regard to this particular form of non-verbal communication. This is because touching, as a major form of bodily contact, has very powerful overtones. Touching another person's body is normally indicative of the degree of intimacy we have with that person and it can range from a simple hand-shake to a sexual caress. In the hairdressing salon and in the doctor's surgery, however, the meaning of a touch tends to be neutralised. Nevertheless, it is probably the case that touching may still be enjoyed as such within the salon both by client and hairdresser. Indeed, for very good reasons it would be somewhat surprising if this were not so.

As infants, our first major contact with others is through touch. We are held closely; we are cuddled, kissed, hugged and generally stroked. But, as we grow up, this form of contact with others diminishes despite the considerable pleasure it gives. There is nothing particularly natural about this. It just happens to be the way our society behaves. We know this because anthropologists have found that there are very wide cultural differences in both the amount and type of touching. In many societies men will hold hands in public while talking to each other, whereas in our society this is restricted to heterosexual couples. In some societies men will even stand with their legs entwined while talking. In one interesting study a psychologist simply looked at the frequency with which heterosexual couples touched each other when sitting in cafes. It was found that in San Juan (Puerto Rico) they touched 180 times per hour, in Paris 110, but in London 0!

It has been argued that in our own society we have so little physical contact with others outside sexual contact once we have grown up, that we are really quite 'stroke deprived'. It is interesting that among the higher species of apes, adults spend a great deal of time grooming one another and clearly derive a lot of pleasure from this activity. Touching is not always sexual. It can be a sign of caring or of comforting. And, of course, it feels good to be cared for and comforted. Even as adults, when badly upset about something, we will feel better if a friend comforts us by putting an arm round us. Even having a bandage put on you by someone is pleasant.

So it should not be surprising if, for many people, having their head touched is a pleasure in itself. Having one's hair brushed and combed or having one's scalp massaged can be a very pleasant sensation. It is probably the case that for most clients there is a distinct pleasure involved in having their hair attended to. It is a legitimate way of being touched. However, although it is the norm for hairdressers to touch their clients, it doesn't automatically follw that this will always be pleasurable. For the very reason that touching has sexual overtones and is something about which we have strong taboos, a woman must feel relaxed and comfortable with her hairdresser. If all of the other components of non-verbal communication do not act together to create a comfortable and safe social relationship between client and hairdresser, then the client may well experience being touched by the hairdresser as distinctly unpleasant. For the hairdresser touching is simply the norm, but for the client it can be either a pleasure or a rather disagreeable experience.

Proximity

Closely related to touch as a form of non-verbal communication is proximity or the distance that you stand or sit from someone during a social encounter. There is a sense in which we are largely unaware of this aspect of behaviour, although we automatically observe the norms which hold for different social situations and will certainly strive to re-establish the norm if for some reason it is violated.

It is possible that there is a biological component to this. We know that very many animal species maintain a territory and will defend it with great ferocity against any intrusion. Humans also seem to display a similar kind of territorial behaviour, although different societies will differ in what is the norm. Certainly, we each of us have an area of *personal space* around our body. This is a zone into which others will not normally intrude and, if they do so inadvertently, will withdraw, often with an apology. The size of this zone of personal space will vary depending on whom we are with as well as where we are. For example, it will be less extensive when we are with friends or intimates than with acquaintances or strangers; in other words, we allow those with whom we feel safest greater access to our person. On crowded buses and in lifts we tolerate strangers much nearer to us than we normally do, but it is noticeable that we adopt a very oblique orientation towards them on such occasions and carefully avoid eye contact, which would normally be concomitant with such proximity.

A violation of one's personal space is experienced as disturbing. Thus we feel distinctly uncomfortable when a bore at a party button-holes us by pinning us up against a wall and maintaining a closer than normal distance. We often characterise as 'pushy' those people who do not observe the norms relating to personal space. The cultural difference in this norm of proximity can lead to some strange behaviour when people of different societies meet. It is known that Arabs and Latin Americans prefer closer proximity than Europeans and North Americans. An anthropologist once observed the behaviour of delegates to an international conference and found that many of them seemed to be engaged in endless gyrations around the floor. What was happening was that Latin American delegates who were talking to Europeans or North Americans were constantly trying to establish their own norm of proximity by coming closer to them than was normal for the Europeans or North Americans. So, the latter were constantly stepping backwards to readjust the proximity. It may well be as a result of a cultural difference in this particular segment of behaviour that we come to hold national stereotypes. Thus, for example, South Americans might well regard us as cold and aloof simply on the basis of the feeling of avoidance which they experience with us. Conversely, we might well see Arabs or South Americans as pushy, solely on the basis of our feeling uncomfortable when they stand so close to us. For managers of salons which have foreigners among their clientele, it might well be advisable to point out to your staff the considerable cross-cultural differences that exist in this area of behaviour. It could prevent the growth of negative attitudes towards clients, which can only be harmful to your business. One way of convincing someone of the importance of proximity is to deliberately stand too close to them, when they are not expecting it. You will find that while talking to someone, it is quite easy to drive them across the room without their even being aware that it has happened.

Another way in which we defend personal space is by the use of barriers. For example, we will use articles of clothing, newspapers, cigarettes and matches as territorial markers in public places such as pubs and waiting-rooms. However, barriers are not going to be very useful in situations where you want to create a friendly and welcoming impression. Many managers have an office and a desk which faces the door. Now, the positioning of the desk facing the door effectively creates a barrier between the manager and whomever he is seeing in his office. The barrier creates a distance and reinforces the manager's status. If you wish to reprimand a member of staff for some misdemeanour or to handle a complaint from a difficult client, you may feel safer behind your desk and you may be more effective. On the other hand, when you are interviewing applicants for a job in your salon or when you are counselling one of your staff on a personal problem, to sit behind your desk will be the wrong strategy. You should come from behind your desk and sit with your interviewee in a couple of easy chairs. This will help create a friendly atmosphere and thus relax your interviewee. A relaxed applicant is more likely to reveal his/her personality than an anxious one and your job of selecting the most suitable applicant will be made both easier and more reliable. It is also worth giving some thought to the reception area. Viewed from the entrance to the salon does it appear as a barrier to a client? Or does it draw the client further in?

Conclusion

In this section we have described some of the social psychological processes involved in hairdressing. In particular, we have considered hairdressing as a form of social construction of self-images. We have pointed out that one major consequence of this definition of hairdressing is to emphasise the importance of the social climate in the salon. We have considered that the impression which the client forms of your salon will be critical in determining whether or not she comes back again. The major vehicle for creating the right impression is the manner of your-self and your staff both towards each other and towards your clients. An analysis of manner reveals that it is made up of a variety of forms of non-verbal communication — most of which is given out unintentionally. It would seem then that the manager who becomes aware of his/her own and others' non-verbal cues is in a better position to improve the performance of his/her staff and to maintain a regular and satisfied clientele.

4. How to Improve Your Interviewing Skills

One of the major tasks of the modern manager is interviewing people. The manager may need to interview an applicant for a new job, a member of staff who is ready for promotion, or a client who has a complaint. These are very different situations which the manager of a salon may face but the skills required are very much the same. Most large companies spend a lot of money and time training their staff in the skills of interviewing because they see this ability as crucial to the effectiveness of their business. There is little doubt that the skills of interviewing are especially important to the manager of a hairdressing salon.

If we take some examples of the situations in which managers of salons may need to interview people, we will see how important good interviewing is to the successful manager. Then we can begin to describe some of the techniques and skills which may help you to improve your interviewing style. Although there is no substitute for experience, as most good managers will no doubt observe, psychologists have shown that some of the basic skills are quite straightforward and much less difficult than they seem. As in a lot of good management practice, if you can put together some basic rules with some everyday experience, you will find that your management expertise will increase considerably. Not only are there obvious business benefits from such an improvement, but your self-confidence and ability to manage will increase so that your personal success and effectiveness will also grow.

Some examples of interviewing situations

A salon manager may face a wide variety of situations in which the skills of interviewing will be of considerable value. Some examples of such situations will help to focus our attention on the everyday problems of the manager. Often the manager will be extremely busy with the other aspects of running the salon and if he/she is also a practising hairdresser, then these problems will be much greater. So it is important that the manager does interview properly, otherwise, as we shall see later, there may be serious difficulties for the business.

Example 1:   A member of staff is having a lot of trouble arriving on time in the morning. They always used to be punctual but have recently begun to arrive later and later. You think that there must be some important personal reason for this sudden change in behaviour. After a while you mention that you are not pleased with this lateness and she then asks to see you about 'a personal problem'. You agree to have a talk. How would you handle this interview?

Example 2:   You have employed a stylist for a number of years and they have become very important to your business. However, although good at her job, you think that she lacks the necessary ability to be a good manger. There is no problem until you decide to open another salon. Because she has been with you for a long time, she expects to become manager of the new salon and has mentioned this to you. Although you have decided to employ someone else as manager, you want to keep this stylist because she is very good at the job. Eventually you agree to see her and 'sort things out'. How would you handle this interview?

Example 3:   A client comes into your salon to complain but you are away. Your receptionist arranges a time for the client to see you. Apparently this is a serious complaint and your client is very upset. The client is important because she has been with you for many years and is very influential in the local community. A bad recommendation from her will have serious effects for your business. How would you handle this interview?

These are just some of the many interview situations which managers of hairdressing salons may face every day. A successful interview can be essential to the profitability of your business. In the first example, unless the personal problem of the member of staff is solved, the manager may be faced with the choice of sacking someone who was a good employee or continuing to employ an unhappy and unsatisfactory person. In addition, the other members of staff may be watching the situation to see how you handle it. Although you cannot be too soft because of the effects on your other employees, you do not want to be too hard because good staff are hard to find.

In the second example, the manager is faced with an extremely difficult situation. If you were this manager, you might want to keep a good stylist but you would also want to avoid employing a bad manager. If the stylist rejects your position, she may leave the business and also convey to other employees that you are uncaring and ruthless as a manager. You want to continue to employ a happy and efficient stylist who will contribute to the success of the business and remain loyal and happy working in your salon. Should you handle the interview badly, you will lose a valuable member of staff, create a bad image of yourself among the other employees and possibly see a number of your clients depart with your stylist.

Finally, in the third example we have the client complaining to the manager, a situation which all managers will have faced at some time or other. There is probably little need to spell out the dangers which face the manager of a salon in this situation. Unless the salon is in the middle of a large city, much of its success will depend on goodwill and the patronage of a regular group of clients. In a small town a bad reputation may often arise because of reasons which have little to do with the quality of the hairdressing. The staff will also be watching to see how you handle the clients' complaints, whom you support and whom you criticise; there is a difficult balance to maintain, for although your clients are the life blood of your business, a happy and competent staff are the foundation on which a successful salon is built.

What is an interview?

An interview is really a more formal kind of conversation. Unlike most of your conversations though, the interview is the way in which you may present the 'image' of your business and an image of yourself. What kind of business do you want to run? Often the only contact which a new applicant for a job or a complaining client will have with the manager is in the interview. What sort of impression do you want them to form of your salon and the type of person you are?

These questions must be taken into account in describing the interview. Although you may think you know the employee who has worked for you for many years, it is often in the interview that the impression of a caring employer or a tough and ruthless manager will be formed. Once this passes into the 'folklore' of your salon you will find it very difficult to change this impression and very difficult to keep good staff.

So the interview is a formal conversation between you as the manager of a business and a member of your staff or a client in which some serious discussion is to take place. What are the rules which will help you to improve your interviewing skills and what can you do to ensure that the outcome of the interview is successful both for yourself and the interviewee?

The problems of interviewing

Of course, there are many problems with interviewing. Some of the most important of these difficulties will be discussed in the following pages. First, however, the interview will only be as good as both interviewer and interviewee want it to be. For example, if one of your employees comes to an interview determined to lie to you about their reasons for lack of punctuality in the morning, then there is little that can be done in an interview to resolve any of the problems which may explain the lateness. If the manager does not have the skills required for good interviewing, then the interviewee may find that the interview has been a complete waste of time. Instead of being able to talk about the reasons for her lateness, she may find the manager spends most of the time talking about his/her experiences when he/she was a junior. Consequently, the employee leaves the interview with no solution to the problem and is likely to feel even more upset than before, so that her lateness may increase. Eventually, more serious action may be required of the manager because of the failure to resolve the simpler problem at the original interview.

Having the right skills for interviewing can allow the interviewee really to talk about the problems which are worrying them. The interviewee, especially if it is a young junior, will often feel very anxious before an interview. Some basic techniques will reduce this anxiety and enable the interviewee to talk. Further skills may allow the interviewee and the interviewer to reach some common solution to a problem, if there is one, or at least come to a satisfactory conclusion which leaves both parties committed to some positive action. A bad interview is where either the interviewer or the interviewee has been prevented from giving important information and where the conclusion is unsatisfactory for both parties.

When is an interview useful?

Although the interview is used a great deal by modern managers, it is also important to realise that the interview is not always the best solution in solving managerial problems. For example, in selecting a new employee you may not find out enough to make an adequate judgement by interviewing or even by administering a hairdressing test. It may be very difficult to discover whether the new recruit will 'fit in' to your salon and many businesses now invite prospective employees to come and work for them for a day or a week, and sometimes longer, to find out whether the person will be happy working for the company and whether the employee will meet the requirements of the business.

The interview is useful, however, when you need to formalise the conversation, as for example, when a client is complaining. Rather than discuss the complaint while you are in the salon, most managers realise that it is far better to take the client into the office, or even out for a cup of coffee, in order to discuss her complaint. Also, you can find out a great deal about a person's reasons for working badly or arriving late in the confidential and quiet setting of the office. Even in recruiting new employees you may learn a great deal about the individual's motivations and ambitions by careful interviewing. In many ways the interview remains the manager's most effective way of dealing with formal conversations with a client or a staff member.

Creating the right conditions for good interviewing

Whatever the nature of the interview most of the skills required are basically the same. However, the *context* or setting of the interview will often be very different and this will have a great influence on the manager's approach to the interview. For example, in some interviews, perhaps in a selection interview, it is important to create a friendly and relaxed atmosphere. Much of the success of the interview will depend on whether the manager can create this atmosphere. But, if the purpose of the interview is to issue a reprimand to an employee (for instance, for being continually late) then the creation of a friendly atmosphere will not lead to the successful outcome which the manager wants. Indeed if there is a friendly feeling at the beginning of the interview, it will be extremely difficult to give a warning which will be taken seriously. If the manager does give the reprimand, the employee will see the manager as two-faced, first being friendly and then becoming autocratic and dictatorial.

Thus it is important to create the right setting for the interview. The *purpose* or reason for the interview will determine the

The wrong conditions for a good interview

setting and the way in which you should approach the interview situation. For example, if the purpose of the interview is to warn an employee about lateness, the manager will make it clear from the beginning that the interview is being used to consider a very serious matter. It is also important not to mix purposes, or objectives, in the situation of the interview. If the manager wants to give a warning to an employee for being late, then this is what should be done; if, however, at the beginning of the interview the employee asks if she can discuss the reason for the lateness, which is a serious personal problem, it is vital that the manager recognises that the purpose of the interview has now changed. The purpose of the interview, if the manager agrees to discuss the personal problem, will not then be to give a warning but rather to listen to the employee's problem. If the manager still wants to give a warning, then he/she should arrange another interview. If he/she attempts to give the warning after listening to the employee's personal problem, the employee may well feel, perhaps with some justification, that the manager does not really care about their personal difficulties. The result may be a very unhappy employee who will avoid coming to discuss personal problems with you on any future occasions; furthermore, this may be communicated to the rest of the staff who will also be unwilling to come to the manager with their personal difficulties. Eventually personal matters may interfere with the running of the salon to such an extent that the manager may be powerless to prevent the deterioration of the business.

Thus the manager who wishes to develop skills at interviewing will ensure that there is only *one* purpose for the interview. To help the manager to be clear about what he/she wants from the interview there are a number of questions which can be asked before the interview begins:

(1) What is the purpose of this interview?
(2) What do I want, as the manager, to achieve at the end of the interview?
(3) What do I want the interviewee to feel at the end of the interview; what message do I want the interviewee to take away at the end of the interview?
(4) How does this particular interview fit into the relationship between the interviewee and myself as the manager (for example, if this is the second interview in which I have had to discuss an employee's lateness, do I need to be more severe in my warnings)?
(5) What is the best way to achieve the objectives which I have set for this interview?

Preparing for the interview

As with many aspects of successful management, the planning before the event will often determine the success of the activity. The degree to which the manager prepares for the interview will have a major influence on whether the interview is eventually successful. One of the most important tasks for any manager before an interview is learning all the background information. For example, in a selection interview for a new member of staff, the manager will need to be familiar with the application form or references and with the details of the job which the interviewee hopes to fill. Unless the manager knows all the details of the job, for instance, he may forget to inform the applicant about an aspect of the job which is only discovered when the person begins work. (At the trivial level, the new applicant's job may involve making coffee, but unless she has been informed of this before she takes up the job, she may feel cheated and annoyed by such a menial task.)

If the manager fails to learn the necessary background information, not only does he risk giving the interviewee a misleading impression during the interview, but also during the interview itself the interviewee may often become annoyed with the manager's inability to be clear about the details of the interview. For example, in the selection interview, if the manager has to keep searching for the interviewee's references or for details of previous job experience, it will soon become apparent to the interviewee that the manager does not really care about the outcome of the interview. The manager will thus have created, often unintentionally, the impression of an employer who is too busy to take an adequate interest in the people who are working in the salon.

Good preparation is essential for effective interviewing. Planning for the interview may involve reading all the paperwork and learning the major points, becoming acquainted with all the details (for example, finding out how the client's complaint originated) and facts which have given rise to the interview and having some clear objectives in mind. Knowing the paperwork or the background to the interview will help to give a much clearer *purpose* to the interview and enable the manager to achieve the outcome he/she wants.

The physical setting of the interview

The physical setting in which the interview occurs plays a major role in determining the success of the interview. In recent years, much psychological research has demonstrated that the physical surroundings in which people work and live can have important effects on how they feel and think. The decor of the salon may have a great influence on whether people feel that their hair is being properly treated. Equally, in the interview situation, how the interviewee feels about the interview will often be determined by the physical conditions in which the interview takes place.

Some salons do not have offices in which interviews can be held and managers are often forced to deal with matters in the back of the salon or in the staffroom. It may often be more effective to take the interviewee, whether a staff member or client, out of the salon altogether, perhaps to a local restaurant or cafe for a cup of coffee. It is more likely that the interviewee will then feel that she is important enough to deserve this treatment and will consequently be more positive about her approach to the interview.

If the salon does have an office in which the interview can be held, then it is important to ensure that the physical setting in the salon office will contribute to the successful outcome of the interview. It is much more effective to talk to the interviewee in easy chairs which are next to or at right angles to each other and which have a small coffee table in between, than to conduct a confronting conversation across a desk (which may be covered with paper and dirty coffee cups!). Preventing any incoming telephone calls and unannounced visitors will ensure that you can give your interviewee the undivided attention which the interview deserves.

In modern business the manager's time is valuable and interviews can use up a lot of this scarce commodity. If the manager intends to interview, it is worth while ensuring that the interview is conducted with the maximum effectiveness. By creating an easy and relaxed atmosphere, by giving time and attention to the interviewee and by providing the right kind of physical setting, you are demonstrating to the interviewee that you see the conversation as being of considerable importance. Such efforts may have a great impact on your business. For example, in the selection interview it may be the only occasion on which the interviewee comes in contact with your business: what kind of image do you create? Do you appear as a concerned and caring employer, someone for whom people would want to work and someone who runs a 'good business'? The interviewee may not be given the job but may be a potential client, or may communicate her feelings to friends, a fact which may determine whether you recruit efficient staff or attract new clients.

Similarly, in giving staff appraisals (that is, letting your staff know how they are doing) the manager will want to create the impression of an employer who is concerned about the staff and who takes an interest in their careers and their personal happiness. Managing in the salon will be easier if the image you have created among your staff is of a caring employer. Also, in interviews when you are helping staff with personal problems, the physical setting may play a crucial part in determining whether the employee opens up on the personal difficulties. There is little doubt that the effective manager who pays attention to the physical setting of the interview and the details of the conversation is more likely to have staff who will be content and happy in their work. Ultimately, it is this side of the business that the client will see. A happy and efficient staff may convey to the client the same image that the manager has presented to them. Thus the investment spent in ensuring that the physical setting of the interview is right may often pay much greater dividends, even outside the interview situation.

Non-verbal communication in the interview

The topic of non-verbal communication is dealt with in chapter 3, but it is very relevant to interviewing. In recent years research has shown that much of what we think and feel about other people is determined not so much by what they say as by what they do. Making sure that you communicate to the interviewee on the non-verbal as well as the verbal level is central to the effective interview. Just as in ensuring the right atmosphere by creating the right *physical setting*, the manager needs to pay considerable attention to the non-verbal information which is being given to the employee or the client. It is not an effective strategy to listen to an employee's personal problems with a bored look on your face nor is it helpful to yawn continually. (This rather simple example demonstrates the way in which what you are doing may often reveal how you feel to the other person without realising it.)

In the interview setting the importance of ensuring that the non-verbal communication is creating the right image cannot be over emphasised. Creating a 'comfortable' distance between manager and interviewee, encouraging the interviewee by head nods and smiles and the use of gestures, may all contribute to the total impression which the interviewee forms of the interview. The manager needs to focus as much on the non-verbal as on the verbal communication, if he/she wishes to achieve the objectives which have been set for the interview.

The interview itself

The interview has been described as a special kind of conversation. Because it is special, we need to pay particular attention to the *roles* of the interviewer and the interviewee. For example, when the manager interviews an employee he/she must be aware of the special relationship which exists between the two parties in the interview. As the manager, you have all the power to decide when to begin the interview, what will be discussed and when to end. Often in deciding on their objectives for the interview, managers forget that the interviewee will also have some objectives. If the interviewee also does not achieve the purpose of the interview as he/she sees it then there will be a feeling of dissatisfaction at the conclusion of the interview.

One of the simplest methods by which the manager may try to take account of the interviewee's objectives is actually to practise the interviewee's role prior to the interview itself. You can sit where you intend the interviewee to sit, and then attempt to answer some of the questions which you will put to the interviewee. It is only by this exchange of roles, putting yourself in the place of the interviewee, that you can begin to comprehend the feelings and thoughts of the interviewee facing you. For example, is your chair higher than the interviewee's, so that she has to look up at you during the interview? Is it difficult to maintain easy eye contact without developing neck strain? These minor irritants, which may have a considerable effect on the way in which the interviewee experiences the interview, can be foreseen and prevented by simply placing yourself in the interviewee's position. After practising these skills for a while and actually changing physical positions, you will automatically take into account the feelings of the interviewee. Once you have attained this level of skill, many of the qualities demanded of the effective interviewer will fall easily into place.

The right conditions for a good interview

The content of the interview

Because time is one of the manager's most valuable resources
it is essential that the interview does not become an endless
chat. The interview should be carefully limited in the amount of
time which the manager wishes to allow for the session. One
method of limiting the time is to have a specified or set number
of items to cover. Clearly, planning is of some importance in
deciding which are the important issues which must be covered.
For example, in the job selection interview when you are interviewing new applicants there are certain types of information
which you must communicate to the job applicant (for
example, the content and conditions of the job, the skills you
require and the career prospects you offer) and there are also
certain kinds of information which you must find out from the
interviewee (for example, the applicant's personality, previous

experience, and expectations of the job). Because it is essential for the success of the interview to communicate this information, time spent on discussing irrelevant or less important matters, such as modern fashions, may not be time well spent. If you wish to elicit broader types of information, it is best to arrange either further interviews or perhaps an all-day visit to your salon. The golden rule, therefore, is to decide on the time you have available to interview and to establish what precisely you will need to communicate and to find out during the interview. Having determined your schedule, be sure to keep to the plan, otherwise you will seriously overrun the time you have allotted or you will have to conclude the interview before all the relevant communication has occurred. Because the manager is the interviewer, it is his/her responsibility to work out the content and structure of the interview. Failure of the manager adequately to control the interview will leave both interviewer and interviewee with the feeling that the interview has been a waste of what is, especially for the manager, a valuable commodity, namely time.

The process of interviewing

As we have said, *the manager,* as the interviewer, *has the responsibility of making the interview a success or a failure.* So the manager must always be in control of the interview. When the interviewee enters the office for the interview, she will, to some extent, be somewhat anxious and concerned about the nature of the interview. It is the manager's job to alleviate this anxiety and to relax the interviewee so that the content of what is said will give a true impression of the interviewee's thoughts and feelings. One technique which the manager may use is to begin the conversation, after the initial greetings, with some general but brief topic of conversation; for example, 'Have you had any difficulty finding us?' or 'Nasty weather today.' Although this general conversation will help, it is also important that the manager conveys the correct non-verbal impression. If the manager is sitting behind a big desk and summons the interviewee in, directing her with a wave of the hand to some small chair in the corner of the room, then the interviewee is unlikely to feel sufficiently confident to give a true impression of her abilities and characteristics. Ultimately, the manager should want to gain a true impression of the person being interviewed: if the interviewer fails to create the right conditions then he/she may employ someone who is inadequate for the job or, conversely, may turn down an applicant who might have made a major contribution to the business. Although the examples that have been chosen to illustrate the rules of interviewing generally refer to job selection situations, the broad principles of interviewing apply whatever the purpose of the interview.

So, the initial part of the interview is best used in relaxing the interviewee and ensuring that she feels comfortable and confident. However, it is important to realise that five minutes spent discussing the weather in a thirty-minute interview are five precious minutes wasted. While it is important for the interviewee to feel relaxed, it is also important not to waste any unnecessary time. The manager, being in control, should then state the purpose of the interview; the interviewer should check out with the interviewee that they both agree on the objective of the interview. Discovering after half an hour that the applicant has come for a permanent job and that you only want someone who is temporary or part-time is a major failure on the part of the manager.

The next important step is to agree on the *conditions* of the interview. Perhaps you need to say that the content of the interview will be confidential, especially if it is a personal problem that is to be discussed. You may need to say that the interviewee can smoke or, because it is just a preliminary meeting before you test salon skills, that the outcome of the interview will not decide whether she will be offered the job. When the manager has clearly stated the conditions and checked out that the interviewee has understood them, then it is important to agree a finishing time. This is critical because the interviewee will often not know how much time there is; if she expects to have an hour with you and suddenly discovers after half an hour that the interview is over, she may not have said many of the important things which she wanted to say. Finally, the interviewer needs to state the agenda of the interview, what types of areas you want to discuss and what kind of information you want to give and receive. This will give the interviewee time to prepare, and thus the answers which the interviewee gives to your questions will more likely be a true reflection of her feelings or thoughts than some quick response off the top of her head.

The interview can then begin and much of its structure will be determined by the purpose or objectives which have been stated. For example, in the job selection situation the manager may continue by describing the job, the conditions which the new employee will have to observe and the career prospects which the salon can offer. In dealing with a personal problem, the manager may simply want to ask the employee how she is 'getting on' and then sit back and listen carefully to any problems. Whatever the purpose of the interview, it is important that the interviewer concentrates on ensuring that the non-verbal communication which is being received by the interviewee does convey the impression of someone who is concerned about what the interviewee is saying. This may involve simply relaxing yourself, maintaining eye contact and perhaps smiling. Whatever you do, it should conform to the purpose which you have defined for the interview; thus, in considering an employee's attempted explanation of continual lateness, the manager should convey the impression of the seriousness with which he/she views the matter – in this context, smiling would be inappropriate.

The most important feature of the interview is whether *accurate* information is being communicated and received. It is critical that both the interviewer and the interviewee have sufficient time to say what they feel and think. Because the manager often depends, in making decisions, on the information received during the interview, *the good interviewer should plan to listen more than he/she talks.* Once the manager has communicated the information that he/she wants the interviewee to know and has checked that this has been received and understood, he/she should then allow the interviewee to have her say. To borrow a well-known phrase, the interviewer has two ears and only one mouth and should therefore listen twice as much as he/she speaks.

This then concludes the opening sequence of the interview and much of the success of the rest of the interview will depend on the skills which the interviewer possesses. As was stated earlier, much of the skill of the effective interviewer is the product of experience and often of having made many mistakes. But the simple rules which form the basis of this experience may be described. It is up to the individual manager to attempt to learn and *practice* these skills, so that the interviews which he/she conducts will serve the objectives of the business in the most effective way.

The skills of interviewing

Because the manager needs to find out what the interviewee really thinks and feels, he/she needs to encourage the interviewee to talk as honestly as possible. By asking *exploring* questions the manager can begin to understand how the interviewee sees things. Exploring questions are those to which there is no right or wrong answer and no simple reply. The manager can develop this skill by asking open-ended rather than specific questions; for example, in the job selection interview the manager might ask, 'Why did you go to technical college after you left school?' (which encourages the interviewee to explain some of the reasons for her behaviour) and not, 'So you went to technical college after you left school?' (to which the answer is simply 'Yes' and the interviewee is unable to explain some of the factors which are important. The use of specific questions ('You worked for two years in Blogg's salon?' rather than 'Why did you work for two years for Bloggs?') should be reserved only for checking out information (for instance, on an application form).

Another skill which the interviewer requires is the ability to *listen actively*. The importance of this skill cannot be over-emphasised particularly because it seems such an obvious part of interviewing. Unfortunately, the skills of listening are much harder to attain than they apparently seem. Perhaps, the easiest way of explaining this paradox is that many interviewers are left at the end of the interview with no clear picture of the person they interviewed. They can recall a number of facts but they are unable to draw any clear conclusions. Their judgments are consequently often based on a few facts which may do little justice to the interviewee. The skill of listening should therefore be practised constantly. One method is to build up a picture of the interviewee as the interview progresses: what kind of person is she, will she fit, what are her motives, and so on? Identifying the 'melody line' of what is being said rather than picking out isolated points will contribute to a better understanding of the interviewee's position.

Building up a picture of the interviewee can be helped by identifying *the critical incidents* in the content of what the interviewee is saying. Thus in the job selection context it may be the reasons for leaving a previous job or beginning a new job which you need to identify. These incidents can then be explored with open-ended questions: for example, 'You say you left Bloggs after two years, can you tell me why?' Such questions enable the interviewer to reach a much better understanding of what motivates the interviewee, what the problems are likely to be if she is employed, or what level of skill can be expected. By identifying critical incidents, asking exploring questions and then following these with more probing questions (for example, 'You say you left Bloggs because you didn't get on. Can you tell me more about this?') the interviewer can begin to build a comprehensive picture of the interviewee. Equally, *critical omissions* may tell the interviewer as much about the interviewee as critical incidents: for example, the interviewee's avoidance of explaining why she has not gained her qualifications after so many years.

When the interviewer thinks he/she has a clear picture of what the interviewee is saying, he/she should *summarise* what has been heard and check out with the interviewee that this summary is accurate. This process has a number of advantages: first, it enables the interviewee to confirm that the picture the interviewer is drawing is accurate and this will strengthen the degree of confidence with which the interviwer can make any later judgements. Second, it will confirm for the interviewee that the interviewer has been listening carefully to what has been said: this will encourage her to continue to share thoughts and feelings about the purpose of the interview. Third, summarising what the interviewee has said enables the development of the interview to proceed on a strong foundation with few, if any, misconceptions about what has been said; thus the interviewee will not be upset by hearing the interviewer ask a question which she has already answered. Finally, in recalling the content of the interview afterwards, the interviewer has some very clear points on which to hang recollections and on which to base judgements.

In using the skill of summarising to check understanding between interviewer and interviewee, it is often useful to *quantify* what the interviewee has said: for example, 'You say you left Bloggs because you weren't paid enough, you had few career prospects and you had to work long hours, is that correct?' Turning into specific pieces of information what the interviewee has said will strengthen the summaries as reference points in the interview. This may be specially important if an inconsistency arises later in the interview: for example, 'You say you don't mind working long hours and yet earlier you said that this was one of the reasons why you left Bloggs.' It is also important in summarising to use the interviewee's own words, since this avoids any confusion about the meaning of what she has said and confirms the feeling that you have been carefully following what has been said.

Once again, it is worth emphasising that the good interviewer will be listening to the 'music' of the interview as well as to the words which are actually being spoken. Does the interviewee's non-verbal communication suggest anxiety, particularly when you ask certain types of questions (for example, about the previous jobs held)? What is the message which the non-verbal signals are communicating? Is the interviewee relaxed and confident? If she appears nervous, what can you do to help her relax? It is important to remember that the primary purpose of the interview is to communicate accurate information, so that both parties in the interview can make correct judgements. When someone is nervous, it is unlikely that they are telling the real story about their thoughts and feelings. It is the responsibility of the interviewer to take control and ensure that the interviewee can give a true reflection of their abilities. The non-verbal communication will therefore tell the good interviewer a lot about the feelings of the interviewee.

In addition to the non-verbal communication, what the interviewee actually says is obviously important. For example, is the picture emerging from the interview of a job applicant who has had a series of jobs and has failed consistently to make a success of any of them; or perhaps it is a picture of a very talented individual who has been unable to find the right place in which to improve her skills? Do I want this person in my business or can I provide the right atmosphere in my salon so that the applicant will feel committed to the business and to the development of her skills? By grasping the major themes in what the interviewee is saying, the manager will be in a much better position to make judgements at the conclusion of the interview. So, good listening demands that the interviewer pays attention both to the non-verbal and to the verbal communication and that the underlying themes, the 'music,' of the interview provide a background to the questions that are asked and the final assessment that is made.

Clearly there are many other skills which the effective interviewer requires. Many of these can only be learned by experience, for every interviewer will have different abilities and different limitations. However, one of the situations which most interviewers face, especially managers, is the problem of dealing with negative emotions, particularly when members of staff use the interview to bitch or complain about other employees. Here the interviewer is in a difficult position. The first rule of interviewing is to listen well and not to interrupt the interviewee, but if the manager does react in this way, he/she may be faced with a very difficult situation. If he/she simply listens, then the employee may pour her heart out, feeling that the manager is on her side. If the manager does appear to agree, then the employee may be convinced of support for her view and perhaps take action against the other employee. Such a situation may arise when a junior complains about a stylist. The manager may not want to upset the stylist and yet he/she has appeared to agree with the junior; if the manager fails to do anything after the interview the junior may well feel betrayed and communicate your two-facedness (agreeing with her in the interview and then doing nothing) to the other juniors, so that before you know it you have even worse problems.

The manager might, however, choose to disagree with the junior in the interview itself. But the junior will see this as taking sides and will probably stop telling you anything, so that any future interviews will be useless and her behaviour towards you in the salon may be less helpful. There is an even greater danger in the manager appearing to agree at the beginning of a personal complaint and at the end disagreeing. The interviewee may well feel that you led her along just to find out how she felt, perhaps so that you could tell the person about whom she is complaining. The interviewee in such a situation will feel extremely bitter and resentful: a situation which a good manager will want to avoid at all costs. So what can the manager do in such a case? You cannot agree and you cannot disagree, and the consequences for your business if you are seen to do either, can be quite disastrous!

At the very beginning of the interview the good manager will have decided on his/her objectives, the 'purpose' for the interview. If the manager does not want to hear these complaints, he/she should stop the interviewee before she goes too far. For example, if the junior says that 'The stylist is very bossy' the manager may reply with, 'Well how do you get on with the other juniors?'; immediately the bitching session is avoided and the interview is directed along a different course. This will occur especially when the manager is already aware of the feelings between the junior and the stylist but for good reasons does not want to, or cannot, do anything about it at present. Preventing the interviewee from going too far will obviously depend very much on whether the manager is listening very closely to what the interviewee is saying: hence the absolute importance of good listening. Again it will also depend on the interviewer having a clear purpose for the interview so that he/she knows immediately that this is not something he/she wants to hear.

What if the manager does want to hear what is troubling the employee? How can he/she listen and still not appear to agree with the interviewee? The skill that is required here is the skill of *reflection*. The good interviewer reflects by hearing clearly what has been said, turning it into his/her own words and then repeating it to the interviewee. For example, the interviewee says that 'The trouble in this salon is that nobody tells you anything'. The manager cannot agree with encouraging the interviewee to go further and list all the many problems in the salon and yet expect the manager's support at the end: if the manager disagrees, the interviewee feels criticised and becomes bitter and defensive. The good interviewer will hear that 'The trouble in this salon is that nobody tells you anything' and if he/she wants to know more, he/she will turn this into his/her own words and reflect it back as, 'You feel you are not being told enough of what goes on?' Putting the problem as a question enables the interviewer to remain objective and yet indicate to the interviewee that the message has been clearly heard and understood.

There is little doubt that the skill of 'reflection' is one of the most difficult to acquire. Although it appears easy, there are very many dangers. A bad reflection can make matters much worse than no comment at all. For example, instead of reflecting, 'You feel you are not being told enough of what goes on?' the manager may reflect badly and say 'You feel people are hiding things from you?' A bad reflection will convince the interviewee that not only is the manager not listening to what she is saying, but is also twisting everything. The results of the interviewee feeling about the interview in this way are obvious and cannot be over-exaggerated, not least in the effects which will occur when the interviewee has the opportunity to tell the other employees about the interview. There is no doubt that there will be little trust, an essential aspect of good management, if there are bad reflections during interviews. So while the skill of reflection can be a great asset during the interview, it must also be exercised with great care and control.

To conclude this section on the skills of interviewing it may be useful to repeat some of the most important skills which have been identified. It is critical for the interviewer to have a clear purpose in mind and to list objectives — the things that must be achieved by the end of the interview. The art of listening is perhaps central to the success of the interview; the good interviewer will be listening both to the verbal and the non-verbal communication in the interview. He/she will be identifying the themes in what the interviewee says and the music which underlies the ways in which the message is being communicated. During the interview the effective interviewer will summarise what the interviewee has said and check out that this is the correct information. By identifying critical incidents, and critical ommissions, the interviewer will build the basis for the development of the interview and for the later recall. Finally, in the use of such skills as reflection the true art of interviewing is demonstrated so that both interviewer and interviewee can communicate accurate information and feel, at the end of the interview, that the meeting has been worth while and useful.

Recording the interview

It is often very important to have some permanent record of what has been said during the interview. Unfortunately, taking a lot of notes may often distract both the interviewer and the interviewee. If the interviewer is busy taking notes, he/she will not be listening to the interviewee with sufficient closeness to pick up all the information. He/she will not be able to focus on the non-verbal communication which the interviewee is revealing. Equally, he/she will not be able to send the appropriate non-verbal cues which will tell the interviewee that the interviewer is really concerned about what the interviewee has to say. On the contrary, the constant taking of notes may tell the interviewee that the primary concern of the interviewer is not to help the interviewee but simply to take notes. It is much better to attempt a full record of the interview immediately afterwards. Hence the importance of the critical incidents and summaries, because they will help to structure the record of the interview and make the memory's job much easier. It is also useful to try to use the interviewee's own words. This prevents any confusion about what was actually meant and if there is a future interview, it enables the interviewer to repeat to the interviewee her actual words. This tells the interviewee that the interviewer was listening very closely and is really concerned about what she has to say. It may also be of great value in situations of disagreement: for example, if the employee has promised at a previous interview that 'I will *never* be late again', then it obviously strengthens the manager's position if these words can be repeated to the employee at a later interview which is to be concerned with lack of punctuality.

If there has to be some note-taking during the interview then it is better to stop the interview briefly, perhaps saying, 'That seems an interesting point, I'll just make a note of it.' Unfortunately, if the interviewee sees the manager making a note of a particular item, then she will believe that those are the sorts of things which the manager wants to hear. Therefore the rest of the interview is likely to reflect this belief as the interviewee tries to think up as many similar situations as possible to the item which the manager noted. The best course is to make a full record immediately after the interview. It is important to include time for this activity when the initial interview is being planned. If the manager plans a half-hour interview then five or ten minutes should be added for the writing-up afterwards. Many managers neglect the recall stage altogether and prefer to rely solely on their memories. Unfortunately, over time memories change and the manager who does not make any written record may often be simply creating a great deal of trouble for himself at a future date. Once a manager becomes skilled at writing a brief account of the interview this task will take a lot less time than busy managers often claim. The value of a permanent record may not often be realised until a serious situation occurs: for example, when an employee comes to ask your further advice on a serious personal problem several months after you last discussed it and you have forgotten all the details. Needless to say, the interviewee will feel upset that you have forgotten and you will waste much valuable time in repeating the same details. Keeping a permanent record of client's complaints may help to identify long-term difficulties which your salon faces. It is also clear that such records, particularly where they refer to staff problems, should remain confidential and be locked in a place to which only you have access.

How to end the interview

It is important to end the interview properly. Psychological research shows that often people only remember the last few things which happened in an interview and decide how they feel about the interview on the basis of the ending. So the manager should seek to make the ending of the interview as pleasant and as positive as possible. If he has just issued a warning to an employee, there will be little pleasantness but at least both interviewer and interviewee should feel positive about the future. The manager can achieve this by first, recapping both positions – interviewer and interviewee. This will involve repeating the major points of the interview and again the skills of summarising and identifying the critical incidents will help to make this recall easier. When the manager has checked out that the interviewee agrees with this summary, he/she should then explain what happens next and when. For example, in the job selection interview the manager may say, 'Well we have a few more people to interview, but I should be able to write to you next week and let you know whether you have the job.'

It is also useful to ask the interviewee if she has any questions. Often the interviewer is so busy asking questions that he/she forgets that there may be some questions from the other side of the table. When any problems have been resolved, the manager should repeat what will happen now so that the interviewee has no doubts about the next stage of the process: for instance, 'Well you have agreed to make a special effort to come in on time in the mornings and I shall be watching to see how you do. Perhaps we'll have another talk in a couple of weeks to see how you're doing.' Finally, as we said at the very beginning of this chapter, the manager is in control and should therefore take the initiative to conclude the interview, perhaps thanking the interviewee for coming, and escorting her to the door. Interviewers often either end too abruptly, which leaves the interviewee feeling confused and upset, or they linger on the doorstep until both parties become bored. A clear and decisive ending leaves both interviewer and interviewee feeling that the session has been successful and that any future action can be approached positively.

What to do after the interview

As we have already said, writing up a record of the interview is a major priority after the interview. The interviewer should attempt to recall all the major points of the interview, using the summaries and the critical incidents, and ensuring that as many of the interviewee's own words as possible are used. The next stage is to carry out all the necessary actions which the purpose of the interview involved or which the interviewer agreed to at the end of the interview. If the manager has decided not to employ the person then he/she should note the evaluation and write to the applicant informing her of this decision. If the manager has agreed to take some action in the salon, either as a result of a client's complaint or an employee's protest: then this should be done as soon as possible. People often judge others on the speed with which action is taken and managers cannot afford to be seen to be slow in taking action when action is required.

Conclusion

In this chapter we have not attempted to list all the skills of interviewing. Indeed it is unlikely that such a list can ever be compiled because, as with many managerial skills, there is no substitute for experience. However, some of the major principles which, when combined with practice and experience, can lead to more effective interviewing have been outlined and described. Although the setting of each interview is very different, many of the skills are the same. Perhaps the most important of these skills is the ability *to build a rapport* with the interviewee, so that the interviewee feels she can trust in you and confide her thoughts and feelings. Unfortunately there is no one skill or single secret to building a rapport. Rather it is the combination of all the skills we have described, plus experience and several other factors which defy simple description. It is often said that the good interviewer is born not made. This is of little consolation to the modern manager who must carry out a great many diverse tasks in managing a business and yet still find time to undertake interviews which may have very great influence on the success of the business.

The message of this chapter is that we can take some simple measures to improve considerably the skills we already possess. A checklist of these skills is provided as a guideline to the effective interview. But the real skill in improving your interviewing techniques is the constant re-evaluation of how successful the interview has been. *What did I do this time which I shall try to avoid next time?* A good method is to cast yourself in the role of the interviewee, just as you did before the interview began. How will the interviewee feel as she leaves the office? Will she feel reassured or confident that she has said all that she wanted to say? Will she feel confident in your decision, knowing that at least you have *listened* carefully to what she had to say? What could you do at the next interview to increase the interviewee's positive feelings about the interview? Unless the manager is constantly seeking to improve these skills, as in all the skills of managing, it is likely that he/she will settle for something which is less than the best. In today's world the manager who settles for anything less than the best is unlikely to be the manager of a growing and successful business. The art of interviewing is one of the foundations on which the effective manager will build success.

How to end the interview properly

Interviewing skills checklist

Purpose: Be clear about the purpose, strategy and objectives of the interview; both as you see them *and* as you think the interviewee will see them.

Plan: Obtain and be familiar with *all* the necessary documents and information. Check that you have allowed sufficient time and that what you want to achieve is reasonable within these constraints.

Physical setting: Structure the physical environment so that it creates an easy and relaxed atmosphere; this should characterise the whole interview and will communicate to the interviewee that you *care* and *understand.*

Interview: Learn and practise the skills of interviewing; they include:
    building rapport;
    listening;
    exploring;
    exchanging accurate information;
    summarising and checking out;
    controlling the non-verbal communication.

Termination: Always conclude with a clear plan of action. A commitment by both interviewer and interviewee to act as a consequence of the interview is the sign of success.

Act and review: If you have undertaken to act, do so as soon as possible. Always review the process and outcome of the interview: did you achieve your objectives? What would you do differently next time? Try to simulate how the interviewee might feel and perhaps check this.

Conclusion

Although this book is segmented into chapters, you will have gathered that many of the concepts are interrelated and to a large extent depend on the support of each other. Take, for example, the concept of 'gain and loss of esteem'. The initial attitude you convey to others is influenced by the 'first impression' which you create through the appearance of yourself and your salon and this, in turn, is mediated by the 'non-verbal signals' which you give out. All these factors are going to be of importance in the interview situation, where your initial attitude is formed.

One of the major problems, and for some the fascination, in trying to analyse human interaction is that the outcome of a situation very rarely depends on one factor alone. It is the same in hairdressing, where a hairstyle is very rarely the outcome of a single operation: cut, curl, condition and colour are usually interrelated and the experienced hairdresser manages to blend each operation, so that its contribution to the final result cannot be consciously estimated, it just becomes a part of the whole. However, having said that, there is one very important factor in the operation of your salon on which will depend the whole success of your business. The factor is YOU; and it is hoped that the success of this book will ultimately be reflected in its ability to make YOU more proficient in handling human relationships.

Your client, for example, needs to feel confident in the work that you are doing in creating the most important aspect of her life. Her identity, her image and her appearance are all created by you. She must be made to feel the most important person in the world. She must be reassured that you care. But if she assesses from your non-verbal communication that you don't care, then no matter what you say, she will form a bad impression of your salon. If she communicates this to her friends, then your business will suffer. So, on your training evenings you could begin at a very simple level to instruct your staff in the importance of their non-verbal behaviour. This would improve the quality of the service to the client. Similarly, by improving your own non-verbal skills, you can improve your own relationship with your staff. In so doing, you will increase their commitment to your business and their service to your clients.

Of course, the results you obtain from applying any of the concepts discussed in this book may not be immediately noticeable. Like any skill, proficiency comes with practice. So, *consciously practise* and use this book as a manual. Dip into it now and then to refresh your memory. As we saw in the section on memory, you cannot hope to remember everything — so don't expect to. However, with practice you will soon discover how much easier it becomes to apply the principles which have been outlined in this book. So use it. I hope it brings another dimension to your Successful Salon Management.

Further Reading

Chapter 1

Gahagan, J. (1976), *Interpersonal and Group Behaviour* (London: Methuen).
Gregg, V. (1976), *Human Memory* (London: Methuen).
Reich, B., and Adcock, C. (1976), *Values, Attitudes and Behaviour Change* (London: Methuen).

Chapter 2

Cook, M., and McHenry, R. (1978), *Sexual Attraction* (Oxford: Pergamon).
Knapp, M. (1972), *Nonverbal Communication in Human Interaction* (New York: Holt, Rinehart & Winston).
Laver, J., and Hutcheson, S. (eds) (1972), *Communication in Face-to-Face Interaction* (Harmondsworth: Penguin).

Chapter 3

Argyle, M. (1978), *The Psychology of Interpersonal Behaviour,* (Harmondsworth: Penguin).
Argyle, M., and Trower, P. (1979), *Person to Person: Ways of Communicating* (New York: Harper & Row).
Aronson, E. (1980), *The Social Animal* (San Francisco: Freeman).
Goffman, E. (1971), *The Presentation of Self in Everyday Life,* (Harmondsworth: Penguin).

Chapter 4

Argyle, M., and Trower, P. (1979), *Person to Person: Ways of Communicating* (New York: Harper & Row).

Banaka, W. (1971), *Training in Depth Interviewing* (New York: Harper & Row).

Higham, M. (1979), *The ABC of Interviewing*, (London: IPM).

Sidney, E., Brown, M., and Argyle, M. (1973), *Skills with People. A Guide for Managers* (London: Hutchinson).